WOMEN, DECISION MAKING, and the FUTURE

Barbara Barksdale Clowse

John Knox Press
ATLANTA

Library of Congress Cataloging-in-Publication Data

Clowse, Barbara Barksdale.
  Women, decision making, and the future.

  Bibliography: p.
  1. Women—Conduct of life—Decision making.
2. Woman (Christian theology) I. Title.
BJ1610.C57   1985   158′.1′024042   85-18091
ISBN 0-8042-1137-X

© copyright John Knox Press 1985
10 9 8 7 6 5 4 3 2 1
Printed in the United States of America
John Knox Press
Atlanta, Georgia 30365

CONTENTS

For
Elizabeth and Henry Barksdale
who taught me to face the future.

INTRODUCTION

A woman whose lifeline coincides with the past two decades of historic change sometimes feels that she is confronting chaos. She also realizes that she is being offered chances. Living in a pivotal generation, women are developing intellectual and spiritual attitudes that will integrate with economic and social changes. Today women know that, more and more, a secure future depends on their own actions, choices, and judgment. They face situations unknown to their mothers and grandmothers. They are forced to make decisions that contemporary men do not encounter.

Decision-making techniques offer women a promising way to deal with contradictory expectations and to take advantage of new opportunities. A contemporary woman makes countless decisions throughout her lifetime. Many are minor and go almost unnoticed. Others are significant choices requiring careful handling in order to succeed. The decision-making procedure described in this study is applicable to small everyday matters and complex dilemmas. In every case decision making demands time and thought, but the effort will vary according to individual preference and importance of the decision. Sometimes a woman can resolve a question in perfunctory fashion. In other situations the process may be long and arduous.

Decision making is depicted here in four steps that are analyzed in chapters 5 through 8. The preceding four chapters offer readers some background for the process. Step 1 of the procedure is called Establish the Givens. It gives the effort some structure and helps to define the pending decision. In Step 2 a decision maker tries to identify all the possible alternatives through investigation and, perhaps, expert advice. During Step 3: Envision the Outcome, a woman visualizes the results of her decision making. This step alerts her to obstacles as well as possibilities. In Step 4 she takes action, making certain that she gives the extra effort that is often necessary to a successful outcome.

Greater skill at making decisions fits with the new realities of women's lives. The following pages contain many examples of women in the process of deciding. I have often chosen illustrations of serious, complex choices in order to make the material more helpful. It is significant that many of the individuals portrayed had no alternative but to act. This emphasis on forced decisions is intended both as an appeal and a warning to make fundamental choices directly and early. Chapter 9, which focuses on the role of courage in decision making, may prove helpful in this regard. The last chapter suggests how women's decisions in both private and public realms are being influenced by a new view of the future.

Working on this project has given me a unique opportunity to blend knowledge with experience. As a professional historian and teacher of Women's Studies, I understand causes and effects of recent socioeconomic changes. However, I am not just a scholar describing changes in detached fashion but also a woman who has struggled with the impact of change on her life. The material in this book grew out of my own dilemmas and those other women have shared with me in memorable conversations. Although I have respected the confidentiality of these talks by changing identities, I want to acknowledge their importance to the study. An individual reader may find in these chapters only a few points that relate to her situation. If any insight or suggestion helps to deepen her understanding and strengthen her choices, then my attempt to combine learning with commitment will have succeeded.

1

PRESENT-DAY PRESSURES

Contemporary women of all ages voice a strong sense of change and uncertainty. "I feel like I've been shot out of a cannon," one woman observed, "and I have no idea where I will land." Another described a sensation of being "sent on a long trip but not furnished with road maps. Then they removed all the highway signs as well." A third woman complained, "All of the rules have been changed, and I can't get a copy of a new rulebook!"

These reactions are typical of women in this transitional generation. Many are hopeful. Even more are confused. Questions keep coming; answers seldom follow very easily. Women ask: should we try new lifestyles? readjust relationships? We see ourselves in a new light, but how do we get men to share the vision? Undreamed of possibilities exist. What about all of the obstacles? Why do we look at our lives and relationships so differently now? Are recent changes temporary? What can we expect to happen next?

Partly, these questions flow from generalized uncertainties about the future. For instance, U.S. economic problems weigh on all citizens. It is hardly clear, however, what to do about these problems. During the past decade inflation was complicated first by stagnation, then recession. Most households felt directly the impact of both trends. Living costs rose, as did the number of layoffs. Wage increases failed to keep pace with expenses. White collar employees saw declines in their real purchasing power and wondered what lay ahead for them. Anxious wonderings of farm families climaxed in foreclosure and auction. Clouds of worry darkened the lives of factory workers who read about industrial robots and clerical employees who heard of computerized offices.

Still, many questions relate specifically to women's lives. Obviously, women have always felt steady, sometimes overwhelming, pressures. Presently these seem worse. A contemporary woman of any age can be heard to complain that she feels "up against it." A twenty-two-year-old woman told of having struggled to complete her education and obtain a job. These were no small feats. Now she wanted to get married. "How can I be both wife and worker," she asked, "with no 'wife' of my own for support? Should I complicate life further by having children? What will happen to my job performance if child care is a problem? Is a second paycheck really worth all that I have seen working mothers go through at times?"

Marriage does indeed seem to be a vulnerable, unstable institution. One marriage fails for each that endures. "I've been looking at myself as a personal tragedy," admitted a young divorcee, "but I'm just another statistic. Do you realize that the divorce rate has more than doubled since 1960?" Aggregate figures are as gloomy as the rate. In 1965 there were 479,000 divorces in the United States. In 1981 that figure had risen to 1.2 million. "I am not yet thirty years old," this woman continued. "I could have half a century of living ahead. Today, though, I feel more devastated than liberated." She went on to describe how hard it had been to lose all her presumed economic security.

The young woman's problems were compounded by having to look for a job. She was not qualified for those she wanted and finally settled for something less just to stay afloat financially. She had to establish credit and financial resources of her own. Like many women, she was completely unprepared for the sharp decline in income level, often as much as 50 percent, that follows divorce. Divorcees of all ages are shocked to learn that, under a no-fault divorce law, the family home may be sold in order to divide equally the proceeds from liquidating this major asset. Women in this situation may never be able to afford a comparable residence again. Regardless of the basis on which property settlements are made, statistics show that females face increasingly poor prospects following divorce. Many women endure long-term hardship.

Married women in their middle years also feel a sense of unsettledness and sometimes frustration. A housewife of forty-two said, "I wish we could go back to the good old days when every woman was home minding her business and you knew it was going to stay that way. There are times when I think my head will burst if I hear any more about crises, shortages, computers taking over the world." Her agitation subsided a little, and she concluded, laughing, "What I'd really like to do is turn the marketing over to my husband. That man refuses to believe I can't feed us with the same dollars he was giving me three years ago. I know he hasn't gotten a raise, but the supermarkets haven't heard yet!"

Older women as well express anxious thoughts about the future. "My husband is retiring," commented one, "from a job that's been his whole life. I don't know whether we can adjust to our new situation or not. He hasn't prepared himself, and I can't imagine having him in my little domain all the time." A widowed friend reminded her, "Just be thankful you have him at all. I'm not only lonely but afraid in my empty house. I heard on the news that America's elderly population will have increased two and a half times by the year 2040." She heard correctly. Even during the 1980s the nation is expected to have a 15 percent increase in the sixty-five to seventy-four-year-old group and a 30 percent rise in the age category over seventy-five. The widow sighed, "What will become of all of us?"

Such questions, which typify concerns of contemporary women, deserve answering. As will be seen, the answers are taking shape. For example, the widow might be encouraged to know that current research efforts promise to revise dramatically Americans' perception of what it is like to grow old. Investigators are delving into all aspects of the elderly experience. Although they are still in early stages of understanding the decades beyond age sixty, researchers report that many expectations are false. A woman need not anticipate reduced vitality, senility, or decrepit behavior. At age fifty a contemporary woman can often look forward to years of energy and vigorous activity. A middle-aged daughter joked with friends over her elderly mother's latest needlework that announced, "If I'd known I was going to live this long, I'd have taken better care of myself." The reality is that many women are going to live more than eight decades. The final third of life can be very active.

Preventive action does seem called for on several fronts, but how does an individual begin establishing control over her life? The biggest obstacle to living more purposefully is the daily blur. Women especially have difficulty overcoming present-day pressures. To begin with, they are so busy today. "Look at my family's calendar for this week," a working mother said. "Just tell me how I'm going to make it to next Saturday. Could somebody like me ever plan the future?" Also, until recently few women were raised to believe that their future was subject to their control. The idea that the future could be whatever they made it was foreign to women in the past, and many still hesitate to embrace the possibility. Tired and uncertain, they hope the worst will not happen and try just to hang in there.

A woman's first task is to rise above the daily blur. She starts by putting recent socioeconomic trends in perspective. Once she sees that tens of thousands are experiencing similar predicaments, she may be encouraged to think differently about her particular status quo. With some background and understanding, she may move to plan her future. Knowledge precedes informed action. A woman may feel inwardly that she should change something about her life yet lack intellectual grounds for doing so. If she understands what is happening to her entire generation, the insights could influence her own thought patterns. When someone warns her that it is wrong to tamper with rightly ordained roles or assures her that age-old ways are best, she will know why such views will not do. Once she comprehends all the forces shaping women's lives, she may gain confidence to move out, make a fresh start.

What has happened in the past decades to cause women to sense that everything is different for them? The basic force behind these changes is economic. Women are in the labor force to stay. Actually, women have been going to work since World War II. Urgencies of war required that all the population give full effort. Women responded by handling many jobs usually done by men. In 1940 women constituted 15 percent of the work force. Contrary to popular belief, after V-J Day they all did not simply return home. Between 1947 and 1980 the number of working women grew by 173 percent. At every age, out of need and by preference, women are seeking employment. In 1980 more than half of all adult women found some work outside the home. The fact that 62 percent of married women with school-age children were then employed highlights a profound underlying change in attitude during the postwar era.

More than three-fifths of all married couples now report that each partner is employed although many wives work only part-time. Census studies reveal dramatically why more and more married couples desire two paychecks. In marriages where both spouses work, the wife's earnings (even from partial employment) boosted family income by 30 percent to an average of $28,636. Researchers project that by 1990 only one in four married women will be a full-time homemaker. Over several decades women have come to view themselves as one of the family's potential wage earners. This perception has led to a long-term trend that is unlikely to reverse. Married women tell researchers they prefer paid labor outside the home to uncompensated work as housewives for a cluster of reasons that cannot be ignored or oversimplified.

In addition, most women who are presently on their own must seek employment. Census data showed that more than 25 percent of adult women headed a household in 1980 versus 15 percent in 1950. Two-thirds of these families consisted of women with children under eighteen. In fact, between 1960 and 1984 the proportion of American children living with one parent grew from 9 to 25 percent. Increasingly, these households are falling below the poverty level. In 1984, for instance, average weekly earnings of married couples were twice as much as those of families headed by women.

The poverty rate for families headed by minority women with children has soared above 50 percent. Such families hope to break out of poverty and welfare dependency through gainful employment, but the process is not easy.

Women must also chart the political climate in order to grasp another explanation for their impression of change. The U.S. political atmosphere warmed to change considerably around the mid-1960s. Anyone who remembers the succeeding decade hardly needs to be told that political transformations occurred. In particular the cause of minority rights flourished. Yet it is as easy to overlook the longer perspective here as in the economic sphere. More than is realized, the dramatic developments of the sixties and seventies had been germinating for many years. Since 1945 America has been a very different nation from that of prewar times.

The civil rights movement aimed first to realize legal equality for Black Americans, then women made a parallel demand for equality. Feminists reappeared on the political scene. What was the relationship between the two movements? Did the former cause the latter? And, in what sense? Were the same Americans involved in both causes? Did politicians treat each with similar seriousness? Have these two groups made comparable progress in their drive for legal equality and economic opportunity?

Researchers are as yet much too close to the two movements to answer all these questions fully. One fact about causation is worth remembering, however. Since the antebellum feminists linked efforts on behalf of slaves before the Civil War to endeavors for their own rights, it is hardly surprising that the causes were again connected in the midtwentieth century. Demands by Blacks in the 1960s generally opened the eyes of women to their own status as "niggers" in American society.

The civil rights movement provided women with rhetoric, an ideological framework, and some firsthand experience. As Blacks and liberal white supporters protested against unfairness and inequality, the women recognized that they were not equal either. Some gained knowledge of protest techniques and a taste for activism in the civil rights movement. From the employment statistics cited earlier it should be obvious that increasing numbers of women encountered job discrimination just as they were becoming attuned to equality. Consciousness and experience combined, and women began to agitate directly for their own equality.

The cause of equal rights bore rich political fruits during the sixties. President Kennedy's Commission on the Status of Women published its conclusions in 1963, the same year the Equal Pay Act was enacted. The report suggested ways that government could help women achieve a fairer position in American society. This national body stimulated state and local groups to review the cause of women's rights. The commission and the new law were more significant steps than either the federal legislative or executive branches had ever been willing to take.

Women gained other important political victories in Washington. In 1964 Title VII, the equal employment clause of a civil rights bill, was amended to forbid discrimination by sex as well as race. Enacted into law, the Civil Rights Act became the primary means by which the federal government moved against job discrimination. The mechanism of enforcement was the Equal Employment Opportunity Commission. Under steadily increasing pressure from women's groups, the EEOC moved against cases and practices that violated Title VII. With the addition of the Age Discrimination in Employment Act, women who are the victims of either sex or age discrimination may file charges with the EEOC. If a negotiated solution fails, they may file suit against the employer, on whom the burden of proof then rests. This is a time-consuming and expensive way of fighting injustice, but women should realize that sometimes merely serving notice on discriminating employers will cause them to reconsider unfair practices.

The best known watchdog against discriminatory practices during these years was the National Organization for Women, founded in 1966. The body reflected the assumptions and tactics of moderate feminists whose orientation was around government and business. NOW also worked for such political guarantees of women's rights as the Equal Rights Amendment. Successful enactment of an Equal Credit Opportunity Act in 1974 and Title IX of the Educational Amendments Act of 1972 encouraged these "mainstream" feminists to believe that political gains were being solidified in

Washington and numerous state legislatures. The political climate chilled, however, and even moderate demands for child care centers, tax law reforms, and the like came under attack. However, a body of legislation, judicial decisions, and executive orders still exists, providing women with the means to redress wrongs.

Profound socio-cultural upheaval has been a third source of new viewpoints about women. In the sixties, for example, youthful radicals began objecting to prevailing social values. Their protests, directed mainly at U.S. involvement in the Vietnam War, included other aspects of American society as well. The highly publicized antiwar movement fed the new feminism in at least two ways. Anger over the war made many women more sensitive to injustice everywhere. Their objections deepened. Moreover, women encountered a crude chauvinism from radical males who professed commitment to justice, freedom, and equality. Embittered by the contempt of their men, women protesters drew closer to one another and to emerging feminism.

Scholars generally draw a distinction between this development and the movement oriented around political and economic reform. Often labeled "women's liberation," its adherents looked at the cause from a more radical perspective and seldom organized large pressure groups. Instead they adapted techniques and experiences from the student revolts to the cause of women's rights. They used small support groups for consciousness raising. They focused on male supremacy as the root of women's troubles and struggled for means to overturn domination of their sex by men. This social emphasis led them to rearrange personal relationships and try to end traditional "masculine" and "feminine" stereotypes of human behavior. Their explanation for women's subordination also stressed biological functions as the key determinant of social roles. As their label attests, they demonstrated a fierce dedication to personal freedom and control over their own lives. Such attitudes contrasted with moderate feminists' concern with employment and law.

Finally, women's lives have been altered drastically by another new social reality: ready means to control conception. The possibility of determining reproductive functioning for themselves freed countless women from the prime determinant of their foremothers' history. Sexual activity no longer usually led to conception and a child. It was possible to have intercourse without the age-old dread of pregnancy. Not all groups of American females have benefited from this change. For example, in 1980 more than half a million babies were born to teenage mothers. The United States has the highest teenage birthrate of any industrialized nation in the world. Nevertheless, the declining birthrate among married women and its correlation with higher educational levels constitute a significant trend. Having access to cheap contraceptives and legalized abortions gave many women a wholly new set of options in the sexual area of their lives.

Extramarital sex increased for women in every age category. Adolescent girls felt particularly strong pressures. Earlier generations of female teenagers could offer a number of reasons for abstaining: they refused to risk so much so soon; "nice" girls would lose the respect of many boys; they had no contraceptives. Such reasons lost their controlling force in the sixties and seventies. Scarcely after entering puberty some girls began taking the pill, or college girls obtained a diaphragm. Both groups became more sexually active. Older single or divorced women found that abstinence had little currency in the social scene. In short, most women have been affected directly or indirectly by the sexual revolution.

Even a brief review of the most conspicuous economic, political, and social changes shows why women are correct in their impression that the female experience has been transformed. Many forces and individuals have worked to alter American society over the past three decades, but great disagreement exists over what its new structure and general value system should be. Even staunch supporters of women's rights find cooperation to be difficult and divide over complex issues, although the wisdom of making common cause has been demonstrated on some noteworthy occasions. In 1977, for instance, the National Women's Conference held in Houston united behind an impressive array of resolutions touching on many aspects of women's lives. Also public opinion has definitely shifted in a general direction favoring women's rights. When the Harris Poll announced in 1979 that 65 percent of Americans supported efforts to strengthen and change women's status, the findings were a dramatic increase over the 42 percent of a decade earlier.

To complicate matters, throughout this transition Americans' overall understanding has lagged behind the realities which they face every day. One might say that there is a large gap between ideals and actualities. Social scientists would probably tell us that we are experiencing a paradigm shift. What this means is that the informing framework by which all of us understand daily realities is still in the construction phase. Individuals and families hold contradictory expectations about how to live. Attempting to meet these conflicting demands, women often feel torn and anxious. Until the collective consciousness catches up with the new realities, women will be caught in a bind.

The sexual revolution illustrates how ideas lag behind realities. Questions related to sexuality, which have always profoundly affected women's lives, today are more numerous and more complicated. These choices have proliferated for the average female to the extent that she might be tempted to look back upon her grandmother's day with nostalgia (though only momentarily). Whether the decision is to take the pill, bear a child, or receive estrogen therapy, the repercussions are great. Some of the most momentous choices are made when women are very young and barely aware of the full meaning of sexuality. Yet women lack a strong frame of reference in which to make these decisions. An individual has no clear, ready basis on which to say yes or no to a possible sexual partner. Females who adopted the traditional male attitudes toward sexual behavior found that code just as unsatisfactory as businesswomen who tried to model themselves after businessmen.

A second lag between ideas and realities came into being because American females were not—and apparently still are not—socialized to contend with their new circumstances. Time and again women may be heard to complain, "Nothing in the way I was raised prepared me for how I'm living my life." Girls traditionally did not grow up expecting to take responsibility for their own future. Recently (and rather abruptly) women have been offered the opportunity to plan and control their time just as men usually have done. Some have begun to do so even though their new living and work environments and values can occasionally alienate them from traditional friends and parents. Others still fulfill all obligations to their significant others before making any plans for themselves. Many mothers are determined to rear sons and daughters differently from traditional ways. This resolve promises an easing of conflicts over gender roles in the future. Nevertheless, where the deepest ties among humans are involved, patterns of behavior are very resistant to change.

In the meantime, traditionally feminine nurturing goes on. Many female children are still encouraged to be mainly pleasing to others. They grow up depending on others to tell them what kind of person they are or should strive to become without reflecting for themselves about who they are. Such conditioning gives rise, at the very least, to self-doubt. It can lead to more serious consequences when a woman loses approval of her significant others and lacks a clear identity of her own.

Also the plans and decisions of women are still more deeply influenced by family situations than are those of men. Girls expect to assume the primary role on the homefront though the majority of women must now succeed in the workforce as well. They are ready to take far more responsibility for familial relationships of every kind than their brothers are. They have conflicts over the wife-mother and employee roles that their husbands by and large never experience. Attitudes are changing. Nonetheless, many women feel ambivalent or even selfish about doing something for themselves alone.

A third lag arises from sweeping economic changes. Women move into the workforce without a corresponding hope that they will ever find equity in employment. The commitment to equal pay for equal work is as elusive as an ethos for integrating employment with housework. The gap between male and female incomes is wider today than it was twenty years ago as female hourly earnings lag farther and farther behind those of men. In 1983, the Bureau of Labor Statistics reported, women who were employed full time averaged earnings of $260 per week compared to $393 for men. The discrepancy widens at the managerial and professional levels. Today salaried women overall earn about 40 percent less than men.

Equity in employment is also hindered by sex segregation in the workplace. Low-paying jobs such as secretary, nurse, or kindergarten teacher are still filled almost completely by women. Affirmative Action programs mainly targeted higher level openings, but even there their effectiveness has diminished. As long as extremely small numbers of women actually hold jobs equal to those held by men, equity will be denied. Women want to see employers lay aside prejudices and outdated ideas that affect their earnings and advancement. They want a chance to be hired for positions that would produce equal pay. They wish companies to comply with the legal dictum for fair pay. The Equal Pay Act became law in 1963 after being debated by Congress for eighteen years. The first federal legislation ever to outlaw sex discrimination, it is still the only law to deal exclusively with that issue. Provisions of the act have since been broadened to apply to more workers, but, in reality, wage differences have grown.

Women detect another lag in the stance of religious institutions toward these sweeping changes. The church was a stronghold of their foremothers. Even now women would like to respond to their new realities within its framework. They want increased opportunities to share crises and transitions openly with fellow Christians rather than to wear a mask in church. They request more study materials that examine the relationship between Christianity and women's rights. They are realistic enough to know that the church cannot proliferate programs and services endlessly, but they do desire the word of God regarding the transformations they are experiencing with their families.

However, women continue to get conflicting signals from the church. Congregations and often entire denominations have been slow to offer women roles of leadership and influence equal to those of men. Clergy have not always spoken out strongly about the concerns of women within a biblical context. In fact, certain sects and numerous individual congregations are arrayed against the cause of women's rights. They see traditional male-female roles as part of a God-given hierarchy that must be preserved against all challenges. They warn that women's liberation could destroy the family. Ambiguity on the part of religious institutions toward recent social changes only adds to the frustration, and sometimes anguish, that transitional women within the church already feel.

Despite all difficulties, women are starting on their own to close the gap between ideas and actualities. They are finding ways to cope with complicated circumstances. In conjunction with the men and children in their lives, they are developing methods of juggling home and office demands. They have no alternative. Since changes affect so many American families and households, they must cope. Progress will be uneven. Sometimes women simply cannot reconcile claims of a sick infant, a corporation, and a tired, confused husband.

Yet many who work with transitional families at the grassroots level believe they have done far better than society's informing institutions have conveyed. More and more couples are committed to an equitable relationship though they may have very different ideas about cleaning a bathroom or a kitchen. They intend to share parenting despite employer resistance to flextime and on-site nurseries. Families are making it possible for women to claim new opportunities. Individuals and households have adapted, innovated, and managed a new way of living.

Moreover, women are helping one another deal with dilemmas. Lacking role models for these new lifestyles and tried-and-true methods for handling swollen schedules and conflicting outside pressures, women depend on swapping experiences with one another. The techniques are often a trial-and-error variety, but women seize upon this "underground information." They also heed warnings from older women who, reflecting over the years, say they would do differently if they had the chance. The word choice is significant. Too often in the past women's lives were left to chance even in areas of major developments. Women today want to take advantage of opportunities purposefully and not leave the future to chance.

Thus, women can use the decision-making techniques described in this study to good advantage. The changes just outlined have left women with a sense of being vulnerable as well as liberated. Today a woman typically cannot look to men to take care of her as women once believed they could. She must rely on herself.

She has no desire to turn back the cultural clock. She cherishes hard-won freedoms. Replacement of laws supposedly protecting the weaker sex with policies and decisions based on the principle of equality is progress. She welcomes the chance to have an identity separate from father, brother, husband, or sons.

Yet the changes do give women the uncomfortable suspicion that in addition to being offered opportunities, they are exposed to many vagaries as well. Businesses do lay off their female employees without considering what the second paycheck means to a couple. A young management trainee is confounded when the secretaries call her a "cold fish" while male cohorts have ways of reminding her she's not "one of the boys." If she advances, she will face the puzzle of how men relate to a female supervisor. In the home, a housewife on the threshold of old age discovers that decades of devotion can end in total emptiness. A young woman finds that her sweetheart's apparent commitment was pleasure seeking instead.

Finding it neither possible nor desirable to depend altogether on other persons, a woman seeks to secure the future for herself. Her search for security demands decisions. She determines to do whatever is necessary. She sheds false assumptions about the future and quells crippling fears. She takes risks. She tries to shore up the most vulnerable aspects of her life. She acquires the training, the job, the material assets that will produce needed resources. She builds protection against life's contingencies. As she works, her confidence grows. She may be vulnerable still, but she is stronger.

A decision maker is never alone. She hopes to receive support and understanding from other persons. Assuredly, she can draw upon the help of God. The power of God comes to anyone struggling to act wisely, to choose well. Women especially must apprehend that power. Much of the Judeo-Christian tradition is culture-bound and patriarchal, but God is not. God is more than any one individual can or will ever know. Without question, however, God is a force moving in and through women today. Thanks to the power of God and their own efforts, women are making informed decisions that preserve the strong parts of their lives and promise richer experiences ahead.

Going a Step Further:

1. What are the most striking points of contrast between your life and that of your mother? your grandmothers? How do you think your daughter's life will differ notably from yours? your granddaughter's?
2. Which of the socioeconomic changes mentioned in the chapter has affected you particularly?
3. Refresh your sense of the recent movement for women's rights by reading a book such as Gayle Graham Yates, *What Women Want: The Ideas of the Movement* (Cambridge: Harvard University Press, 1975) or Elizabeth Janeway, *Cross Sections: From a Decade of Change* (New York: William Morrow & Co., 1982).
4. Identify the most significant gap between ideals and actualities that exists in your own life. What changes would be necessary to close that gap?

2

THE SCOPE OF
WOMEN'S DECISIONS

Women make many types of decisions. These choices may be
separated into categories for discussion purposes. In fact, most significant decisions come under more than one category. For example, when a divorced mother goes job hunting, she weighs concerns
about family responsibility, financial solvency, and time management, as well as personal development. While a woman's decisions
seldom fall solely in a single category, it may help to take an overview. Perhaps considering the most common decisions classified by
type will prompt a reader to reconsider some aspect of her life. She
may take action on a choice she has been considering. Increased
awareness often does lead to informed action.

A woman's primary decisions lie within a broad category that
might be labeled personal development. These choices and actions
relate to her education, training, vocation, hobbies, health, friends,
lovers. Within this category her special talents and aptitudes deserve early and persistent attention. It is extremely important but
often hard to choose wisely and well about one's abilities. Many

women have found it helpful to begin their planning with the recollection that these abilities are sometimes called gifts. In truth, a person's entire life is a gift from God to be enjoyed fully and used well.

Holding fast to this conviction may inspire a woman to make good decisions about her talents and aptitudes. If she believes that God endowed her with a gift and intended something unique through her life, she is unlikely to give up until she grasps that purpose. If she identifies special aptitudes clearly, she will aim specifically for certain work or pastimes. She takes initiatives about schooling or improvement of talent. This is not a belief that engenders exaggerated self-importance or unrealistic ambitions. It produces, rather, desire and willingness to go to great lengths to find the best way to use one's special gift in glad response to the Giver.

Few women can escape altogether making vocational decisions. In past generations women were identified principally as members of a family, while a female today usually has some status beyond her household. When someone is introduced, an early question typically is, "What do you do?" This query implies gainful employment. As already seen, many reasons now compel a woman to plan for some sort of work experience. In truth, it is best to take a vocational attitude toward all the nonprivate components of life. A woman with vocational vision makes long-lasting commitments to activities and interests. She may outgrow one or add another, but throughout, she thinks of herself as committed. This outlook is appropriate to volunteer work, enriching pastimes, or careerism. It is an attitude of choosing to become involved rather than living year after year passive or indifferent.

Most commonly, people link vocationalism with meaningful employment. Aside from the economic realities, intangible gains accrue from early vocational plans of this type. Having a vocation means that a person takes herself seriously and aims toward competency and responsibility. A vocation can be one way of showing a lot of the authentic self to the outside world. When a woman matches her unique personality with the right work setting, her efforts can be productive and satisfying in ways that few hobbies can match. It is possible to make too much of work, yet life was meant to be taken seriously. Without some significant work at hand, life can become trivialized, even meaningless. One's vocation provides a special continuity to living.

Decisions about health, another aspect of personal development, give a person the zest to keep working. Whether an individual realizes it or not, good health is the foundation of any life. Without it, one's future is not secure. Health choices are more important than financial decisions. A great deal of money does not mean much in the life of one who loses her health. It is often hard to accept the truth that we are responsible for our own health, yet sound decisions in this area of life begin when people assume a stance of control over their health whether they are well or sick. Of course, an individual relies on health care professionals for treatment and her intimates for support. However, it is sometimes necessary to challenge a doctor's judgment, reject a course of treatment, and insist on answers to all the questions. An encouraging sign is that the American Hospital Association has formulated a code of patient's rights that includes getting complete information about a case. Therefore the responsibility truly does rest with each person even if that individual becomes ill and is in the care of an expert.

The realization that God intends for people to be whole and healthy can sometimes be a powerful therapy when one's health stands in jeopardy. At times any person grows weak and opens the way for destructive, unhealthy forces to prevail in her life. In a complex way, someone may even choose to be sick. On such occasions, it is easy to forget evidence of the healing power of God. Through the life and ministry of Jesus come reminders of this joyful reality. Contemporary doctors and nurses set the stage for the healing process to take place. Their efforts cannot succeed without active involvement of the sick individual, yet the process is aided by the same power that intervened in Judea two thousand years ago.

The essential decisions about health are those that help prevent illness and disease. Americans cannot ignore rapidly mounting evidence in favor of prevention. Even simple changes in behavior and diet apparently effect significant improvements in one's general health and well-being. No doctor makes these choices for an individual. Doctors warn their patients. When conditions warrant, they admit patients to a hospital. Yet, short of hospitalizing a person permanently, no doctor can force a patient to follow courses of action that insure continuing good health. Long-term planning is the key. Studies indicate that when Americans learn and follow sound mental and physical health practices, statistics of the killer diseases decline.

Preventive health habits are also cheaper. The cost of treating illness and disease has soared to unacceptable levels, forcing Americans to realize that they pay a very high price for failing to take care of themselves. Recourse to doctors *ex post facto* is a poor option. Both health care professionals and their potential patients desire to seek alternatives to treatment after the onset of disease. The concept of wellness is a promising approach. It shifts responsibility to the individual, encouraging one to choose a lifestyle that minimizes risks to health. Experts say that many of the most widespread and costly health problems in America today could be ameliorated by personal commitment to wellness. Countless men and women have made this a guiding principle of their health decisions. Despite flabby muscles and the apparent presence of carcinogens everywhere, these people are sticking by their choice.

The holistic approach to health decisions includes a dimension other than fitness, diet, or stress management by considering the role played by emotions and attitudes. Several years ago editor Norman Cousins captured the interest of the public with an account of how he employed positive emotions like good humor or laughter to conquer a terrible illness. The book, *Anatomy of an Illness as Perceived by the Patient*, brought remarkable publicity to holism and boosted scientific interest in the medical benefits of laughter, good humor, and joy. Measuring improvements in blood pressure and muscle relaxation, doctors are seeking to learn more about why people feel so much better after laughing. Healing remains a mysterious process, despite great gains in treatment procedures. Joy is one of the emotions that recharges one's life force and forges new connections between body and spirit.

Questions related to sexuality also fall within the category of personal development. A woman's decisions about sexuality are rooted in her childbearing capacity. She copes with the cultural and biological implications of this reality from the time when as a girl, she realizes that she can give birth to another life. To be sure, biology is no longer destiny. Most American women do not face the prospect of pregnancy every year. Still, the ability to bear and nurture children remains central to women's experience. A female soon realizes, moreover, that her body and health will be more drastically affected by sexual choices than a male's will be. Good decisions about one's sexuality rest on self-awareness, a sense of freedom, and faith in one's future time.

Nowadays a woman's sexuality imposes choices on her from puberty onwards. When a girl begins to develop sexually, she usually has some idea of the changes that puberty brings. She learns what to expect physiologically. Someone could even have discussed the emotional transformations she will experience. Yet no one may have pointedly informed her that a succession of decisions regarding sexuality lie before her. Before she realizes what is happening, she may come under pressure to be sexually active. At this age she cannot possibly foresee all the consequences of her decisions. If a girl has been encouraged to think hard about who she is and what kind of person she is becoming, she can put that self-awareness to good use. She can ask, "Is the choice I am considering consistent with what I know about my self?"

Confused teenagers face unenviable choices. Whereas once the stigma that sexual activity brought was sufficient basis for deciding, that ethos has changed. In fact, mores have altered to the point that chastity sometimes has come to be a stigma rather than the opposite. Talk at school or on the job may convince a young woman that she is the only pubescent virgin in town. On occasion parents give their adolescent children a jolt unwittingly by offering to obtain contraceptive devices for them or implying that all teenagers now engage in sex. In contrast, counselors of young unwed mothers report that these adolescents sometimes ignored birth control possibilities altogether because they did not wish to face sexual decision making directly.

A woman developing a sense of freedom can use that attribute when trying to make decisions about sexuality. The freedom to make deliberate decisions regarding one's sexual behavior is unique to the human species. Being free to choose, to decide about sex is something that separates humans from species that act on instinct. Unlike other species, humans must accept the consequences of behavior in this area in many complex ways. They cannot blame poor decisions about sex on instinct or uncontrollable feelings, for the gift of freedom of choice does carry responsibilities. On occasion, moreover, it includes the right to say, No, when that is the best choice.

While a teenager may initially view freedom of choice as a burden, it truly is one of God's blessings. The same capability that enabled her to pass school courses, drive an automobile safely, or handle a job successfully will help her make wise sexual decisions. In all cases she is free—to fail schoolwork, to drive recklessly, cheat an employer, or have casual sex. The reality of responsibility means that she must repeat the course, pay traffic fines, could be fired, risks pregnancy or disease or damaged relationships. A sense of freedom will help her make conscious, strong choices in this area of her life as she does in the areas of education, employment, and family relations.

A woman's decisions about sexuality are also linked to her sense of time. Teenagers especially have difficulty understanding that the passage of time will put an adolescent romance in a different light. Moreover, a teenager may not have a great deal of time to make up her mind about sexual relations. As strong feelings sweep through a young couple, they are not likely to go through the decision-making process depicted in succeeding chapters. Assuming that a teenager may decide on the spur of the moment, how can she prepare for a good decision? Besides self-awareness and feeling free to choose, she can try to build faith in her future time. She might begin by considering that the right time for her may not be in her bedroom after school before her parents return from work! She can believe that there really will be more meaningful times ahead to fulfill sexual desires. She starts to envision a rich intimacy that encompasses far more than physical relations.

A second broad category of decisions concerns family relations.

Decisions about family matters are influenced and often complicated by current views of that institution. Most Americans are pain-
fully aware of the alarming, pessimistic statistics about domestic
problems. The family seems to be an embattled entity. It becomes
difficult for a person to believe that her own family can escape
these problems. The public hears constantly from persuasive experts and through the news media what the plight of the family has
become. These gloomy data have a telling effect on people's expectations about family life. It is unfortunate that families have not
been told with equal emphasis that they have coped successfully
with change and shown great adaptability on occasion.

Bombardment of bad news and predictions can serve as a self-
fulfilling prophecy for families. Couples know that 50 percent of all
marriages do not last. Thus, when they hit the inevitable rough
spots, they could be stampeded into considering divorce. Parents
reading about teenagers' sexual mores may reach unwarranted conclusions about the behavior of their own adolescent children. These
parental misconceptions can sway a wavering teenager to make a
regrettable decision. No one can avoid being affected by the cultural climate, and a family may have to choose consciously to go
against common practices or widespread patterns. Its members will
resolve to unite against disintegrating forces. Given a host of difficulties, families have to search for positive ways to counteract
threats and buck the trends.

Two precepts that help improve decisions within family situations are balance and commitment. Families are striving to balance
the needs and demands of all members. They adopt an ideal of
more equitable arrangements. This goal can lead to better decisions
and wiser choices. Equality was the primary objective of the recent
women's movement. Activists worked for change in the public
areas of legislation, court decisions, and economic policy. The private dimension of equality denotes that everyone in a household
will carry equal loads and that the desires of each will be balanced.
Most importantly, a family trying to come into better balance main-
tains close communication among all members.

Families are also using the dynamics of commitment to fortify
their relationships. They recognize that they cannot exist in a vac-

uum or see gloomy trends reverse overnight. What they can do, however, is to say individually and collectively, "This family is going to last." This decision sets the dynamics of commitment going. Family members identify the strengths of their family and try to enlarge on these. They plan occasions that will reinforce their ties. A contemporary family's time together often is limited, but that does not mean it cannot be joyful and special. Depending on their own initiative, families recognize that no societal force will preserve their relationships for them. They also rely on God's truths as a basis for family decisions. Caring unselfish love, forgiveness, and reconciliation are principles that encourage a family to keep the dynamics of commitment strong.

Financial choices constitute a third, and very important, category of personal decisions. Financial security is an individual matter, and this discussion is not a comprehensive look at financial planning. However, the subject is closely related to the themes of the study. Financial security depends to a large extent on one's ability to make sound decisions and take wise actions. Financial choices arise throughout a person's lifetime. Anyone who neglects to set goals, establish priorities, and plan for the future is quite vulnerable. An individual's economic needs change and family obligations fluctuate. The rate of inflation affects one's decisions about how to manage income. Yet the persistence of inflation means that a person must increase income steadily just to stay even. Through all of life's ups and downs the need to make good financial choices is constantly apparent.

A contemporary American's notion of financial security has been shaped by the nation's unique experience. America possessed bounteous resources from the start. Her people historically have counted on a strong material foundation for their lives. After the Second World War this materialism advanced dramatically. With some justification the postwar era has been labeled "the age of affluence." People's expectations grew. In countless households items that once had been considered luxuries became necessities. A significant segment of the population never shared in this economic boom. Nonetheless, the boom did carry millions of jobholders to a higher socioeconomic status. More importantly, the economic ex-

pansion led an entire generation of Americans to expect that prosperity would extend. They based financial decisions on anticipation
of higher future earnings. Children grew up assuming they would
be at least as well off as their parents.

As a result, Americans hold a rather materialistic view of security. When asked about what a secure future means, many give an
offhand definition that it is "having enough money to live on."
They readily add that security also means financial protection
against catastrophes or unforeseen reversals. There is no quarreling
with this basic reality. It sends people into the work force and
keeps them there, however disgruntled they might feel on Monday
mornings. As will shortly be seen, however, the scenario of rapid
economic growth has changed. Easy expectations no longer apply,
especially in women's lives. They do need the resources for daily
living as well as handling the possibility of loss of job, major illness,
property destruction, or problems of old age. Women may wish to
rethink the concept of financial security before formulating goals
for attaining that security.

One can begin by clarifying the distinction between needs and
wants. Many of the trappings of recent times actually fall into the
category of wants. People can live without stereos, televisions, auto-
matic washers, even cars. Yet these possessions are often viewed as
necessities. The primary objective of anyone's financial planning is
to assure that true needs can be met. In the process a person will try
to balance needs and wants. The drive to obtain more and more
material possessions can squeeze real abundance out of one's life.
How can a person rethink the question of needs versus wants?

God clearly cares about meeting the physical needs of human
life. From the Old Testament record and, certainly, from the attitudes and actions of Jesus, one sees that material needs and well-
being are important. A teaching of Jesus recorded in Matthew 6 and
Luke 12 gives a clue to the balancing of needs and wants. He
wanted to set his followers free from unjustifiable anxieties about
everyday living. He challenged them to consider parts of the natural world that lived through the providence of God rather than
through grubbing along. The beauty of birds and flowers can still
remind an overly acquisitive human that it is important sometimes

just to BE rather than striving constantly to accumulate far more things than are actually needed to live. There is more to life than material possessions.

However, life is certainly not much without them. Thus, a woman's first priority is to acquire and protect the means to meet her everyday needs—food, shelter, and clothing. Financial security begins with this capability. Without income to pay for basic necessities, an American falls into the "safety net" of government assistance known as welfare. Its programs range from food stamps to subsidized public housing to aid for dependent children. Welfare keeps individuals from worse suffering, but its complexities, demeaning procedures, and shrinking benefits make it a last resort for many. In 1983, the government claimed, a family of four needed on average $10,178 annually to live above the poverty level. The figure would be lower for smaller households and does vary geographically. It does provide, nevertheless, a sense of lower limits. By comparison, median family income was about $10,000 higher.

Financial security also includes the ability to handle emergency expenses as well as meet the cost of personal catastrophes. Major disasters cannot be met by savings alone but call for the resources of insurance policies. None is more important than hospital and major medical insurance coverage. However, recent estimates are that 38.6 million Americans under age sixty-five lack such insurance. Evidence of growing numbers of uninsured individuals reverses a generation's trend toward protection in this area. The new pattern which has created concern across the nation apparently has complex causes, including unemployment and employers shifting more of the expense of coverage to workers who subsequently drop out of the plan.

Several million middle-aged American women now have no health insurance, and one out of five children is not covered by such plans. The women are too young for Medicare and often do not qualify for Medicaid. Many such individuals have lost access to group health insurance plans but cannot afford to pay premiums of individual policies. They avoid seeking medical treatment until it becomes unavoidable, then they are forced to bear the cost for themselves. Women are coming to realize the steps they must take to gain security against medical disaster. If a woman thinks she will lose coverage under her husband's medical insurance plan and is uncertain of full-time employment herself, she tries to remain in his plan through a conversion right. These rights may be her only alternative to a much more expensive individual policy. Even if she can pay the premiums for an individual policy, they vary greatly and bear careful comparison. Some, for example, pay dollar amounts of hospital costs rather than the more desirable allowance of a fixed portion of such bills.

Women over age sixty-five are learning that Medicare, the federal health insurance program, hardly offers security in this area of financial planning. It covers less than half of an older person's average medical costs and may in the future provide only one-third. Medicare also does not pay the cost of annual physical examinations although these play a key role in health care of the elderly. Specialists in preventive medicine emphasize that checkups detect problems before they become acute or have a debilitating effect on a person who might otherwise remain vital and active. Older women complain, moreover, that some problems (such as hearing loss) for which they seek remedy are not covered under Medicare. When elderly citizens are unable to live independently, Medicare does not pay for "custodial" care in a nursing home. An individual must require skilled nursing care daily to receive benefits. Then the program pays costs of care fully for only twenty days and partially for eighty days. Thus, women must plan to supplement federal health insurance with private policies in order to have security from dreaded illness and financial burdens.

Financial security traditionally has been linked with savings that could be used to meet unexpected or extraordinary expenses. Financial advisers provide clear advice about the importance of having funds readily available in some form of savings account, but they note that the recommendation is seldom followed today. The rule of thumb is that an individual should have on hand for emergencies a sum at least equal to three months' normal living expenses no matter how little that person earns. Those in the financial planning profession find that the advice is simply ignored, especially by younger Americans. Whereas once people saved for a rainy day, now apparently they save to spend. Experts claim that most Americans set aside money only for a specific objective such as buying a new car or taking a vacation, then spending all their "savings." Counselors in this field work very hard to convince clients that all discretionary spending should stop until a minimum of three months' living costs has been set aside and kept for unexpected expenses.

After taking steps to meet regular and extraordinary expenses, a woman plans decisions that will enlarge her control over financial security. While such goals may not seem as urgent as those just reviewed, they merit regular consideration. Any woman who is serious about long-term financial security in today's economic environment husbands her assets wisely. She aims, for example, to reduce her tax obligations to a legal minimum. She uses all of the tax deductions for which she is eligible. She employs income averaging sometimes. She takes advantage of such tax shelters as IRAs and municipal bond funds. Most importantly, she creates a budget tailored to her income and goals. She learns the pitfalls of using credit card purchases to pile up consumer debts. Examining her spending patterns and recalling that debt service should never exceed 10 percent of net income, she may decide to shift priorities and place some wants behind real needs.

Economic developments clearly have great impact on the lives of contemporary women. More and more females are coming to see the need for managing individual financial affairs well and also to recognize the importance of collective action on behalf of economic justice. Such questions go to the very heart of life. No person who lacks material necessities can possess dignity and a sense of worth. Wherever economic injustice exists, that society's well-being is diminished overall. Economic justice was a constant biblical theme through eras of both the old and the new covenants. Contemporary Christians still bear a mandate to act on behalf of victimized, oppressed persons.

Thus, a final category of decisions are those that reflect corporate concerns. Our lives are shared with others. Recognition of this communal dimension of existence by women today often produces strong decisions. Previously, "feminine" gender roles did not call for women to be active in public affairs as a matter of course. The so-called "privatization" of women's lives meant that females typically did not feel that they should participate in the public sphere. Now that "a woman's place" definitely is no longer strictly "in the home," more women are becoming involved in social concerns. The degree of involvement and the issue vary, but a new pattern is taking shape. Women are choosing to have a role in civic life everywhere from their own neighborhoods to the nation's capital. They are doing something about every one of America's many current public issues.

Few would deny that today's problems are serious and that many threaten our assumptions about the future. Some of these forces could drastically affect the fate of humankind. Women are not allowing this reality to short circuit their motivation to take purposeful action, however. They recognize that uncertainty has always been the lot of humans, and they are aware that new issues could dwarf present concerns. It may be, as the saying goes, that "we ain't seen nothin' yet!" Informed women also consider the fact that some notable "problems" are really a result of the revolution of rising expectations. So many circumstances about human life have improved in recent decades that people have enlarged demands and assume that we should somehow bring about further improvement.

Active, committed women are deciding that neither the scale of a problem nor the complexity of a challenge will stop them. None of these troubles is beyond remedy. Each problem came about as a result of human actions and decisions. Only the efforts of informed, determined persons can improve the problems. The challenges will not yield to quick, easy solutions, for they have multiple causes and effects. Yet not a one of these issues—even the perilous arms race—is certain to doom humankind. Sometimes when a person gets interested in learning about a contemporary issue, she feels almost swamped. The rate at which the problem is worsening or the scope of the threat makes her quail at taking action. Just reading about the issue can produce a kind of paralysis of the spirit. "All things considered," one woman asked, "why bother? Could anything I do possibly make a difference?" Solitary concerns will never counter these threats to the future.

However, linking her efforts to those of other committed women will prevent her decision from being stillborn. Collective action lends effectiveness to a cause and also significance to an individual life. When a woman ceases to be turned wholly inward, she grows. Perceptiveness and generosity of spirit increase in someone who has decided to commit time and effort to a social cause. As the common effort advances, these qualities deepen in the lives of participants. This is also how the kingdom of God goes forward. People respond to God's action in their own lives by moving against injustice, suffering, and oppression of all kinds. By such decisions they become God's work in the world.

Going a Step Further:

1. Read The Boston Women's Health Book Collective, *The New Our Bodies, Ourselves* (New York: Simon & Schuster, 1984) or Bruce D. Shephard and Carroll A. Shephard, *The Complete Guide to Women's Health* (Tampa: Mariner Publishing, 1982) for an overview of female health concerns.
2. Develop plans to meet a financial objective such as education of children, retirement, or change of residence.
3. Write a profile of family occasions and activities for recent years. Do some seem to have strengthened family ties more than others?
4. Identify a "cause" that interests you at the community level or beyond. Investigate opportunities for participating and get involved.

3

THE FOUNDATION OF
GOOD DECISIONS

At any age a woman can find herself in a situation where her future depends on sound decision making. A number of attitudes can foster wise decisions. Becoming aware of exactly what is at stake is important initially. This realization can point a woman toward more purposeful living. Second, a woman stands a chance of choosing well if she is straight-thinking and honest about a situation. Third, at deciding times she will want to look below the surface of relationships and let intuition point to possibilities. Fourth, faith in the future will stimulate hope. Shortly we will look at illustrations of each of these four attitudes. All in all, though, the element most valuable to a decision maker is self-knowledge. When making choices, a woman who knows her true self has advantage over someone who is unclear about what she really is like beneath the roles she plays.

A very young decision maker particularly needs awareness. Her knowledge and experience of the wider world is nil. No teenager—however bright—knows the steps to take in securing her future, and she must depend on others to broaden her perception and direct early plans. It is hard for an excited fifteen-year-old who has just learned she made the cheerleading squad to believe she will ever need more than her pompons. With the identity she has claimed, her future seems guaranteed, at least for her high school years. She will have a special wardrobe and visibility. Boys will date her just because she is a cheerleader. What adolescent could ask for more?

This busy young woman may not know that she should reconcile her cheerleading with a growing interest in math and computers. She enjoyed a beginning computer course and had planned to take another one along with advanced math next year. That was before she made the squad. Now her mother's pride and peer congratulations relay the message that she has chosen rightly; done well. Having practiced untold hours and perfected a super smile, she triumphed over losing contenders. She is tempted to forget the math for a while. Most of her friends are not interested in graphs and formulas. Peer pressure on this adolescent is peaking, and few schoolmates know that her math aptitude is higher than her jumps.

It is up to concerned adults to tell the popular cheerleader what the future may hold. If she realizes that in a few years she likely will be working full time, she could adjust her assumptions. Today almost every young female should at least plan on being a breadwinner and strive to assure economic self-sufficiency. Failure to recognize this actuality early has enormous implications for a woman's future security, both financially and psychologically. Being financially independent greatly increases a young woman's flexibility and her sense of choice about everything. Conversely, low earnings potential complicates all parts of a young adult's life. A female may close off vocational options without ever realizing it. The ex-cheerleader could sit down before a computer terminal every morning for many years. The level at which she works may be determined by whether she stays in advanced math in eleventh grade.

Until recently, girls did not grow up expecting to take charge of their future, and parents as well took a different view of male and female adolescents' priorities. They might have worried about sons' economic prospects but more about daughters' peer approval. Now, however, many wish daughters to see that they must have vocational plans and gain a sense of making things happen in their lives. The fifteen-year-old cheerleader can acquire computer skills as well as practicing tumbling. She can make math courses a priority alongside of extracurriculars. If she gains awareness and chooses well, her possibilities for vocational success will remain as bright as her smile.

A further example demonstrates how honesty and realism, along with good information, can make all the difference when one is confronted with a decision. Maintaining a realistic attitude toward circumstances means that a woman is more likely to take advantage of advice and available help. A college senior wonders what she will do when her years of study and work fail to produce a mysteriously wonderful Lifetime Grand Prize. With no real grounds for the assumption, she thought her bachelor's degree would guarantee the future. Her parents are proud of the fact that she is the first family member ever to be a college graduate and equally confident that her diploma will open doors.

Talking with more pessimistic classmates, she feels conflict building. Kindergarten teaching, the only vocation she has ever considered, is in a state of oversupply. A friend tries to persuade her to enroll in a local beauty school and work toward a beautician's license, but she cannot afford to pay for more schooling of any sort. The manager of the jeans shop where she works hints that she might consider entering the franchise's training program. Yet she would have to move often and pick up business administration courses. How can she give up her dream of teaching young children without a try?

Her eight semesters and two summer sessions were pressure packed. She worked part-time at a succession of shops. It seemed to her that going through such effort must be worth a great deal. The harder she struggled academically and financially, the more convinced she became that her reward would be great. It seems too cruel to imagine receiving nothing more at graduation than a piece of paper. If only she had gotten to know the college placement officer sooner. Between her job at the mall and coursework, she has barely had time to think about references and resumes. When asked about her plans, she gives everyone a tight smile and a stock line, "I just haven't made up my mind yet."

This young woman finally decides to accept the harsh realities looming for most new college graduates. They are moving into a changing economic configuration. The economy now is growing far more rapidly at the bottom where openings are for unskilled, service workers than in the middle where many skilled and semi-skilled workers advanced earlier in the postwar era. Midlevel jobs have fallen victim to automation, recession, and the arrival of the postindustrial age.

Along with the growing numbers of women seeking employment, the college senior must be realistic about trends in the workplace and face the problems they create for her. New capital, flowing into high-technology companies, is creating jobs at the top of the pyramid. These positions are closed to all but the most highly qualified females. Lacking the training to obtain high-technology or managerial positions, women are forced to remain at low levels. White-collar and blue-collar opportunities that once might have offered promise of advancement and boosted earnings are not nearly as plentiful. Some of these jobs have vanished permanently.

Once the prospective graduate takes a first step away from cherished dreams, she starts to deal with reality. She determines to explore all of her options. Otherwise she may experience a long and miserable period of being all at sea. She finds plenty of people willing to give information and offer advice. Professors, placement officials, older friends already working, her minister, her boss at the jeans shop figure in the process of gathering information. Then she alone will decide what advice is most appropriate to her situation. Every alternative she considers carries some element of risk. No course of action seems to have a lifetime guarantee attached. Because she has made the mental adjustment from dream to reality, however, this senior can start to secure her future despite the risks involved.

Additionally, the experience of an unhappy thirty-year-old illustrates how intuition can enhance decisions. This housewife and mother is miserable but uncertain how to make a fresh start. She left college after two years to marry her high school sweetheart—a decision she now considers a mistake. The ex-football star today looks more pregnant than she ever did with their two girls. His job at a small local construction firm does not provide the income they would like despite his building garages on the side. They agreed for her to stay at home while the girls were small. Once their younger daughter enrolled in kindergarten, his temper began rising as often as monthly budget costs. She ignores these resentful outbursts because she doesn't want to renegotiate their arrangement but wants to end it completely. Should she trade her old familiar misery for something that might be much worse, however?

Her life seems to consist of endless questions, but she is afraid she will hate all the answers. The girls will soon be gone much of the day, and she would like to contribute more than her labor to the family enterprise. She just cannot contemplate sitting at a desk or standing behind a counter all day. The girls' frequent illnesses have convinced her that she would be a good nurse. The work appeals far more than any clerical or retail job, but training would involve expensive and demanding schooling. She is certain that her husband wants an instant second paycheck. Lately he has hardly seemed like the same person she enjoyed during their four years of dating, though she suspects at times that a different husband could be harder to handle than her grouch. If once they could have half as much fun as in the old days! Now they do not even seem like the sort of couple who remain married for the sake of the children. The girls almost appear happier staying with their grandmother.

Even on her worst days she could not quite bring herself to rupture a relationship that had been central for fourteen years. That instinct proved correct. At the same time, she needed to heed the growing pains she was experiencing. Reluctant to do anything drastic but bursting with unhappiness, she had a conversation with her mother that started a communication chain reaction within their family. All she needed was encouragement to start pursuing her new goal of a career in nursing. Once she could see that her family was a source of support rather than a group of obstacles, her vision cleared.

This woman also found some unrealized assets in her own life.

As she and her husband learned to communicate, they reclaimed strong bonds. He supported her plan to become a nurse. The training was justified by career earning potential. She saw that his bad temper arose in part from the pressure of being their only bread-winner. As soon as she found that all her close relationships had the strength to accommodate change, she could launch a fresh start and direct her energies toward making the new routine succeed.

The entire family learned about the dynamics of commitment. Commitment calls for understanding. No person is perfect. Committed families work at recognizing that truth in everyday affairs. It means setting aside one's pride on occasion, asking for forgiveness, and allowing reconciliation to begin. The decision to admit one is wrong sometimes comes harder within a family than at school or the office. Commitment lasts when family members can see their own foibles and the others' difficulties. Often one person requires much patience from the rest. Efforts do not always even out. Where the dynamics of commitment operate powerfully, family members do not constantly keep score. Commitment can make use of intuitive judgment as in the case we have just examined.

The fourth example illustrates the idea that anyone willing and able to hold out faith in the future will gain a large measure of hope in the bargain. At first faith and hope were the last attitudes that a displaced homemaker felt after thirty years ended so bitterly. At the moment all of her certainties have melted. Deciding what to do next seems an absurdity. Her husband cannot even explain why he left, or at least he cannot offer an explanation that her mother will believe. In fact, her mother acts as if she walked out on her husband rather than vice versa. Their children have usually taken their cues from her. Now they seem to have more sympathy for their bachelor father than their abandoned mother. All of the family loyalties seem topsy-turvy. How can she plan with any confidence?

Moreover, she refuses to look ahead until someone will explain what went wrong with the past. She did exactly what she thought her husband wanted of her by staying home and raising their children. She always believed she was doing a good job with the family. She is determined to find out whether he thought so. Her efforts to talk this out with him led nowhere. She has finally accepted that divorce is inevitable, yet she is obsessed with discovering how the man she married turned into this cruel stranger. She refuses to take one step into her new future until her husband gives an affirmation of their joint past. It does not seem possible that the past thirty years meant nothing, but what is the meaning of that time in her life?

Then an unexpected contact helps her to maneuver the difficult turn away from the past in order to start toward the future. A divorcee whom she knew slightly urges her to visit the Displaced Homemakers Center and learn about the services offered to women like themselves. Slowly she understands her reactions. She was not actually half of a partnership for thirty years. So much of her identity was tied up in her husband that she views herself as a nonentity. Counselors point out that, while it is natural to want to engage in recriminations, she must look to the future. She decides not to spend the next quarter century blaming her husband for persuading her to leave a budding career in merchandising thirty years ago, and she realizes that she cannot keep blaming herself either.

She joins thousands of women being helped to accept the consequences of past decisions and trained to make future ones at a network of Displaced Homemaker centers throughout the United States. She rediscovers the worth of vocationalism. Work can compensate for losses; aid in recovering from sorrow. A sense of vocation structures time and brightens the dreariest of days. She deals with the pain and sorrow of broken intimacy. When a sexual relationship ends for any reason, an individual is tempted to refute it altogether. Nevertheless, the truth of that relationship is valid for the time it lasted, and that love abides in the face of change, alienation, and loss. Eventually the divorcee could affirm the love that had ended. Some faith in the future kept alive her capacity for love.

Finally, a fifth, and often controlling element in decision making is self-knowledge. By reflecting regularly on the questions, Who am I? What is my life all about? a woman lays the groundwork for choices that reflect her unique self. Gaining self-knowledge is a process that never ends but is best begun in adolescence. Early strides toward independence and authenticity set the stage for continued progress in adulthood. If these fundamental efforts to learn about one's self are avoided and delayed, a woman may have difficulty later establishing a purpose in living and feeling somewhat in control of things. A woman who has, throughout her life, considered the possibilities of her special aptitudes and talents is unlikely to wake up one day desolate and overcome with regret over lost opportunities. She may not have succeeded, but she will have tried.

Regular reflections about the meaning of one's life are important for another reason. When troubles arise—as they will—a woman with a strong sense of self will deal with difficulties better. It is sometimes easy to forget that existence is more than the sum total of one's roles and routines. A crisis or troublesome period can thrust a woman into a kind of void. Cut off, even briefly, from the mediating power of her social context, a woman sees that relationships are no substitute for a self. Public and private affiliations are vital. They nourish and enrich all existence, yet a sense of self beneath these ties can carry a woman through a hard time. She knows what her life *in toto* means and has envisaged what it still might be. Such knowledge helps one withstand shock and pain.

A woman can explore a sense of self in many ways. The three techniques to be considered below only begin to suggest possibilities. An individual can tailor them to her personality and situation or devise a different method that suits her. Each of the sample techniques for getting to know one's self are described in turn. The first is through personal history done any number of ways. A woman records her lifeline, identifying significant events and recalling settings that gave great satisfaction, or she writes her biography as an outsider might. The second approach is through silence. These times of quiet meditation may also include brief diary entries or jottings. Third, a woman may gain self-knowledge through the help of small support groups or friends. Although much of the process is carried out by the person herself, small group experiences sometimes move self-knowledge along by leaps and bounds.

Before looking more closely at three approaches to deeper self-knowledge, we should note what women are not attempting. They are not indulging in fantasies. Anyone trying to gain a clearer vision of her possibilities wants to make plans—not have idle dreams. She wants to come into closer touch with life's realities. Second, women are not looking for an excuse to tear apart the fabric of life and try to use a completely different pattern. Working on a personal history should strengthen continuity—not bring on chaos. Most people basically retain the commitments they have made although they may look at these in new and different ways. Taking an imaginary step outside one's roles and routines is a far cry from abandoning everything to live on a mountaintop.

After reflecting, a woman may decide that her life is not all that it might be. She will ask, What is really happening with me year after year after year? Reflection often bathes one's whole life in a new light, giving rise to the desire to change some aspect. One woman recalled, "I began to wonder why I had never considered changing long ago. I saw that nothing really prevented my changing some parts of my life. Questions multiplied. What did the hectic pace that Ed and I kept really mean? Was the kids' endless busy-ness right? We seemed to do everything in a fit of absence of mind." Exploring below the surface, this woman found that she wanted to grow, to change. She aimed in the end for affirmation and fulfillment rather than disappointment and regret.

The most direct way for any woman to begin getting at the question, Who am I? is by reconstructing her lifeline or writing an autobiography. She notes all significant events and then studies the record before her. She can now identify certain turning points though these junctures may not have seemed so at the time. She gets reacquainted with herself at age sixteen, twenty-one, thirty, even older. No person should lose touch with the rich experiences that make up any individual past. A personal history can help a person take hold of hope and find faith in the future. The exercise can be a lifeline in every sense of the word.

Even those who anticipate being disappointed are surprised by lifelines because often more substance is discovered in the record than expected. A woman may find a larger measure of courage than she credited herself with possessing. A person can see her strengths more clearly on a lifeline than she will ever perceive them in the daily blur. Living moment to moment makes it hard to perceive long-term progress. One individual was amazed to see how a painful period looked in perspective. "I couldn't have come through that trouble ten years earlier. I can see that I AM stronger than I was. It was easy to forget this while the pressure was on." Another remarked, "I handled that situation better than anyone else involved. Looking back, I can't imagine myself doing all those things, but I did! I never thought of myself as a take-charge person until now." Achievements become more obvious through writing personal history.

This exercise can be shocking as well as liberating, however. A woman may have to confront for the first time evidence that her existence has been mostly controlled by others. Individual achievements or steps taken on her own seem few and far between on the lifeline. She may wonder if she's been too "nice" to all the others even to consider her self. "My own lifeline is virtually nonexistent!" one woman exclaimed during a discussion of decision making. "I'm somebody's wife and somebody's mother, the PTA's treasurer, the Meals-on-Wheels' coordinator, and a whole slew of other things." When a friend reminded her that she was constantly active, the woman countered, "That's exactly what disturbs me now. I'm afraid I stay in orbit like a crazy comet mostly to avoid figuring out what my life should be about."

Rather than becoming discouraged, a woman should try to look at the record in its entirety. Is there some occasion when she felt fulfilled or managed something well? She can try to recapture the feelings from those occasions and hold onto them as she moves ahead. She accepts that any lifeline has both peaks and valleys. By focusing on a past time when she was afforded genuine satisfaction, she may catch a vision of the future. Past memories definitely relate to future possibilities. Perhaps a woman sees that some youthful dreams do not appear as realities, or she recalls an ambition that she abandoned without realizing. A talent, once remarked upon by family and friends, is missing from the lifeline. The dream, ambition, talent are still part of her. Maybe she has reached the point of deciding to bring that part of the self to fruition.

A second means of beginning the journey of self-discovery is through silence. Carry the process of reflecting to the next level. Learn to create and use silences. Soundlessness is not easily come by today. Most Americans suffer from noise pollution. Sound tracks accompany almost every activity: the dentist grinds away decay to Muzak; shoppers roll along supermarket aisles to programmed jingles and tunes. Houses and apartments reverberate with electronic noisemakers—telephones, TVs, food processors.

One must work at finding a quiet place and the time to learn about silence. Even after hushing the surrounding gadgets, inner tumult must be stilled. It is a struggle to experience silence even momentarily, but the effort is worth it. Once a woman quiets all the plans, recriminations, and fits and starts, she searches out what is deep inside. Her real self is waiting to be found in that silent core. People vary in their liking for this sort of exploration. Some are inclined to stop once they have experienced silence briefly. Others find the technique so interesting that they are willing to journey often to deep, inner terrain.

Experiencing silence can be just as shocking as reconstructing a lifeline. An absolute contrast to habitual noisiness, silence is a strange phenomenon to most women. That is why it can be so revealing. Signals, promises, hints, warnings that are crowded out of ordinary experience may come only in quiet times. Unless a woman clears the way, these clues to being may never reach her conscious mind. Once learned, the practice of silence offers mysterious and wonderful ways of sensing what life is all about. A woman who finds the way into silence should try to keep some of its gifts with her afterwards. She has pen and paper nearby. She writes down anything at all that occurs to her, then holds onto these jottings. She will be surprised at what they can reveal about this self she is seeking over weeks and months.

Often silence is a way to grasp the meaning of relationships. When a home is quiet and empty, walk into silence. Experience the living space of every other person in the household. Are there vital connections among the separate selves or icy barriers? Do the cluttered rooms shelter a whole? In silence a woman sometimes understands the totality of a family. She will know if her self can come and go freely from the others. She will see if she is bound to them by ties that should be loosened. Silence sometimes gives a woman the courage to set her true self free.

Finally, God may come in silences. The prophet Elijah learned this following a confrontation with King Ahab and Queen Jezebel recorded in 1 Kings 19. Elijah ran away from the awfulness of the royal couple in a manner not unlike any modern person's flight from those perceived as enemies. He fled to the cave at Mt. Sinai where he believed that God ordered him out to the top of the mountain. A whirlwind tore everything to pieces, then earthquake and fire climaxed the destruction. Elijah expected Jehovah to come in this demonstration of power. No. Once the devastation faded, Elijah experienced the barest sound that stunned him instantly. Just as God gave the discouraged, frightened prophet a message, the Holy One still communicates in quiet times today. Elijah gained courage and a job to do. In silence, with hearts open to the mind of God, women may yet grasp the mystery of becoming God's work in this world.

Probably it is the element of privacy that makes both personal history and meditation work so well. No one will judge the lifeline or compare it with another's. The thoughts that take shape during silences are not subject to criticism or approval. A woman can give them any form she likes. She thinks or writes about ideas from which she might usually shrink. If she tends to be an other-directed person, she may become free to develop attitudes or opinions that are uniquely her own.

A special kind of release can be found in doing a lifeline or experiencing silence. Either exercise may also point a woman in a new direction. If they prove to be threatening or frightening instead, it may be because the individual insists on judging herself—although no one else does. This reaction is a sign that she should keep at the exercises. It is possible to move beyond this barrier of guilt and self-doubt. Ahead she may find genuine self-acceptance and steady strength.

Although a lifeline, meditation, and other such techniques are private activities, they can be coupled with small group sharing, another approach to enlarged self-knowledge. The day may come when a woman is willing and even eager to explore some of her solitary reflections with others. If she reaches that point, then personal history or meditative jottings will be invaluable. Today many women find it desirable to have an ongoing relationship with a support group of some type. The benefits can be almost beyond measure at any age. Having assured access to a group committed to the well-being of all participants can be crucial at deciding times. This is especially true when the group carefully respects the confidentiality of their conversations.

An isolated woman, perhaps experiencing upheaval, who comes into a group for the first time gains relief from learning that she is not alone in her troubles. Jane's revelation to a new group is typical. "It must just be me," she sighed, "I guess I'm not a very strong person. It makes me so nervous seeing everything unsettled today. I've never told anyone this, but do you know what I'd like to do? Keep my family—this sounds crazy—locked up so they'll be safe. Why can't we avoid the troubles like we used to?" Jane got a tremendous lift from sharing her uneasiness. She learned that unexpected dilemmas and trends had thrown many families besides hers off balance. Other group members sensed problems coming from many directions at once.

One of the remarkable effects of Betty Friedan's book, *The Feminine Mystique*, was that it released countless women from isolation. The book became a national bestseller almost overnight when it appeared in 1963. Friedan provided an explanation for what thousands of middle class women knew only as "the problem that has no name." The reaction, "I thought I was the only woman who felt this way," echoed everywhere in the country. The phenomenal response to the book led to the mistaken notion that Friedan caused the recent women's movement. Actually the book only articulated widespread stirrings of a generation and focused on women's emerging desire to become whole persons in their own right. Friedan made a powerful case for opening up opportunities for women beyond housework and volunteerism.

How does a woman become part of a small group? Perhaps the ideal way is to suggest to some like-minded friends that they form a regularly scheduled body and commit to it. Members might be colleagues from work or neighbors. Small groups often arise naturally among women who belong to the same church, work at a company, or have similarities in age and lifestyle. Sometimes support groups form because women are making the same transition, such as returning to school or divorcing. However, being part of an intergenerational group is a special pleasure. The perspective of older women helps younger members maintain balance. In exchange for this wisdom, the older women receive stimulation and are challenged to try new activities.

What if a woman needs and wants a small group of caring, sharing individuals but sees no ready-made opportunity? She could try attending an interest-oriented group such as community classes or church activities. A support group sometimes emerges spontaneously from shared common interests. If she senses this happening, she can then suggest to others that they become a regular group. An individual who is timid or in very low spirits may not feel she can summon the courage even to ask, not knowing how the others will react to the proposal, though she really has no alternative. When a woman knows that she truly needs this kind of support group, she will have to take the initiative to find one. The rewards can be so plentiful that she will soon forget her panicky uncertainty. The mutuality of a support group strengthens every individual within the circle.

Whatever techniques for self-knowledge a woman adopts, she is well advised to reflect before making a decision. Only after rethinking the question of who she is can a woman formulate strong plans. Even in crisis or when time is short, her choices can then flow from what she knows to be her authentic self. Devoid of self-knowledge, she could take actions that would betray her deepest desires and eventually sabotage her life. The process of learning about and creating a self is lifelong. All people would like to feel that their living somehow made a difference. No woman knows what her lifespan will be. In order to have underlying assurance that her life has mattered, a woman will begin to cultivate a sense of self while she is young. Never again will she have the same opportunity to decide what to make of the life that has been given to her.

With much of their lifeline as yet unrecorded, young women would seem most likely to want to create a unique self, yet they face obstacles to authentic living as powerful as those with which older women contend. Instead of the dead weight of a past, they are imprisoned in the present. Reality for a young woman is that very moment. At fifteen or twenty years of age the texture of her days is so dense that she may never see that she could live more freely. When someone asks, "What are you going to be doing ten years from now?," she can only shrug and admit that she has no idea. If she tries to think about the future, she senses only a kind of void. This lack of framework for the future can squeeze creativity out of a twenty-year-old as completely as regret and fatalism can deaden a fifty-year-old.

Sometimes a girl or young woman starts to live authentically by learning that she truly has been given a precious gift with no strings attached; that she is free to enjoy the gift in every possible way of her own choosing. How different her teens and twenties will be if she has this insight. The insistencies of parents, demands of employers, claims of a lover, and pressure of peers or consumerism do not determine her life. The void that was her future begins to take shape in plans. She finds the satisfaction of relying on her own efforts in purposeful action. She learns not to depend wholly on others for status, identity, or security. She acts rather than reacting all the time. She avoids assuming that others will take care of her; leaving her future to chance.

However, it is never too late. As long as life is granted, a woman can enlarge the meaning of her self. The process can be painful on occasion. It may require giving up some outgrown part of the self and struggling to add a new component. Loss is always painful. The effort may sometimes seem to bring tentative or partial results. More often, however, it is joyous, creative work. A conscious effort to be one's authentic self enlarges life unbelievably. Remembering such times, a woman will know in all honesty that she felt most alive then. Her awareness of both internal and external realities grew richer. She appreciated the special qualities within her and projected that uniqueness to others. She perceived new aspects of people and the environment. As she enlarged her own capabilities, she was able to experience more of life.

Moreover, in the struggle to know and become her true self, a woman often encounters God. Why should so many people claim to have discovered God in their struggles? Perhaps striving to create a self brings one in closest contact with THE creative force in the cosmos. Maybe in times of change and tension, growth possibilities arise for a new relationship with God—the nexus in all creative processes. Also the Holy One becomes for numerous persons the source of their truest identity. Jesus' earthly experience bears witness to this potentiality. Throughout his life Jesus maintained an extraordinary sense of his work and destiny. All the Gospel writers attest to a pattern of solitary withdrawal. During such periods Jesus received from God a clear vision of what his life was to be. That same power comes today to anyone trying to learn who she might become.

Just as Jesus regularly renewed his vision in solitude, so must any woman creating her life. Because of the effort required and obstacles to be confronted, she will need time alone to strengthen her resolve and clarify choices. At some point in every day she should stop and reflect. It is best to set aside a special period—perhaps half an hour if possible—to think about how the creation process is going. This daily attention needs to be deliberate and consistent. Otherwise, she could lose sight of what she wants to become. Jesus is the model. He withdrew to broaden channels of communication with God and make certain of the nature of his work. If a contemporary woman spends a tiny portion of each day reconnecting to that same power, she will continue to grow. However long her span of years, no woman could outlive her potential for spiritual growth. It exists at any age.

The complicated circumstances of women's lives today make it difficult to find a quiet spell of solitude during each day. Pressures pile up. Insistent business crowds out silent, more significant concerns. Since a woman seldom is given occasions for quiet consideration, she must make them. To gain this necessary time she may have to fight a tendency to place herself last in the day's chores. If her special plans appear to be unpromising or her potential for change seems small, she may not feel justified in pushing aside everything else. It takes real determination to disregard a pressing matter or suspend activity for a vision that may never reach fulfillment. It also takes a special form of faith and some courage.

In order to keep her commitment to her future, a woman may

also have to limit her availability at times. Sometimes she will postpone an immediate demand and defer to her self instead. She will learn to put all of her significant others "on hold" temporarily while she considers what progress she is making. To a woman who has become constantly vulnerable to others, a momentary break in every day brings renewal and fresh intentions. Thirty minutes of planning and reflecting each day is far more likely to produce results than occasionally staying up to brood all night when the demands of others have finally ceased.

Women who build such an interval into their days soon learn how much it means to them. Once a woman resolves to make certain that her living matters, she starts to discover what her life should be. She sees that her future has not been determined. She will create it in a sense. This intention means that she must organize, plan, and arrange to give the design a maximum chance of success. Thus, her half hour partly is devoted to the details of planning. Having set her sights on some goal, she must not neglect the nitty-gritty arrangements. In addition to spending moments on necessary organization, she must continue to dream of possibilities. She will keep looking ahead, projecting what her life may become in a year, a decade, a quarter century. Half an hour is a very small part of the present day but a necessary time for a woman who intends to secure the future.

Going a Step Further:

1. Write your obituary or, if you prefer, write a press release on the occasion of your retirement. Are you satisfied with the fundamentals of the account? Tristine Rainer, *The New Diary: How To Use a Journal for Self-Guidance and Expanded Creativity* (Los Angeles: J.P. Tarcher, Inc., 1978) contains many suggestions for exploring the self.
2. Read Wayne E. Oates, *Nurturing Silence in a Noisy Heart* (Garden City: Doubleday & Co., Inc., 1979) and consider ways to build more quiet times for reflection into your daily schedule.

3. Diagram your life, using a circle with each quarter representing twenty years. How do you plan to fill the half-circle represented by age forty through eighty?
4. Read Alan Lakein, *How to Gain Control of Your Time and Your Life* (New York: Signet, 1974). Adapt at least two of Lakein's suggestions to your own situation with the intention of making life more meaningful.

4

WHEN DECISIONS
ARE CALLED FOR

How can a woman be certain that she should launch into decision making? The preceding chapters offered examples of such situations. A woman may come to see that she is at a juncture by her
own reckoning or the observations of others. Sometimes she
reaches a departure point by reflecting and writing down troublesome thoughts that keep recurring. Occasionally the process begins
at the prompting of another person. Habitual conversations and
moods reveal quite a lot to perceptive, caring friends and family
who may observe signs before they become obvious to the individual. In either case, a woman finds herself hovering on the edge of
deciding. Unfortunately, many people do not like to decide unless
forced to do so, waiting until the need for decision making is
unavoidable.

Decisions are often brought about by a crisis of some sort. Although few women may anticipate suddenly having everything
called into question, the experience is not as uncommon as one
would like to think. The status quo can be swallowed up by a single

bit of terrible information. Julie's crisis is described in some detail here by her neighbor and friend. It is telling to see how the nearby shock waves affected the neighbor's thinking. After looking at the way Julie's assumptions about her future crumbled, it would be well to consider how one struggles to make good decisions in extremity.

"Even before Julie reached my house," her neighbor began, "I sensed trouble. When she arrived, her familiar face was a shape I had never seen in all our long years of friendship. I'd been struggling through an uneasy time myself. I dreaded facing more gloom that afternoon. Yet I knew too that I was there to open the door to Julie and let her share the burden with me. I can't remember sitting down— just words pouring out and terrible confusion as I pieced together her day. First to her own doctor's office, then to a specialist who scheduled scary tests immediately. A week of waiting lay ahead before she would know. We used strange terms that could not possibly apply to Julie. Or could they? She did not dare to hope. Neither could she quite believe what might be happening inside her body.

"What I recall most clearly about that conversation was her sense of betrayal. Not fear of pain or debilitation. Not even dread of death if it came to that. What Julie most wanted me to understand was that she could be robbed. Deprived of idle dreams, strong assumptions, vague plans, and fond hopes. Her entire future was suddenly not out there at all. Over and over she cried bitterly, 'If I had known.' Those four words were still echoing in my mind when I woke at four the next morning and crept downstairs in the dark.

"Away from my sleeping family, I reflected over the afternoon. How could God do this to my friend? I thought harder. Dark thoughts. How could I presume to protest to God? There are four and a half billion people on our tiny planet. Billions of stars in the Milky Way and galaxies without measure. I recalled the images of Psalm 90. God just sweeps people away. They're like the dream we know we've just had but can't remember. The woman who had sat through PTA with me, stopped me from dyeing my hair, goaded me into exercising could vanish like last week's grass clippings. I shivered and wrapped the quilt closer around me.

"I wondered, 'Suppose it had been me?' How would I react if illness swallowed up all the years that I expect to have? I knew that I was no different from Julie. I too assumed there was a lot more time to come. We shared Robert Browning's belief that 'the best is yet to be.' Was there any way I could avoid having to repeat those words 'if I had known' should I face what Julie did? I was just as vulnerable as my stunned neighbor. I too was counting on having a great future. Suppose that future were snatched away? How could I possibly then say, 'It's all right. Amen. So be it.' Was my life so far what it should be, or were there many things I ought to have done differently?

"Alone, cold, in the dark I let myself suppose that everything were called into question, as it might be. I made two discoveries. One was what had happened to me by taking my life for granted. I had forgotten that everyday routine may be obliterated by accident, embolism, or stroke. I had presumed that the dreaded disease would always strike someone far down the street or in the next pew. My sense of blessing was dulled. So was my sense of wonder at how hard mere survival can become. Second, I realized that no future is actually 'out there.' Everyone's future—including my own—could be anything imaginable. Only time would tell."

Having to make decisions in the midst of crisis presents special problems. If a woman accepts these conditions, she may eventually find that troubles also present unexpected opportunities. First she reconciles herself to some cold facts. She understands that the story will have no happy ending. The trouble is not going away. It is natural to want to turn aside and avoid unpleasant possibilities; a woman in a crisis cannot. She knows she is on the spot. For instance, a wife in the process of being divorced found that people were not going to be nice. Her estranged husband viewed their relationship quite differently than she did. His attorney was intimidating. Her mother was unsympathetic. In the preceding example, Julie was told that she might have a life-threatening illness. She gave up the illusion she had shared with most healthy people that sickness might wreck the familiar pattern of life but probably not anytime soon.

Decisions made during this difficult period will be complicated by a new kind of fatigue. It is a degree of tiredness never known before. When coupled with anxiety, it seems overwhelming. A woman doubts she can keep going under the dual strains. Her ordeal is barely underway. The road ahead seems long, yet she has already exhausted her usual energy. How can she deal with all the problems at hand, much less those as yet unforeseen? Never before has so much pressure been directed at her alone. She feels this aloneness almost as acutely as she senses tiredness. Both the divorcee and Julie felt wholly separated for a time from healthy or married women who seemed to go about their business unaware of this exhausted person in their midst.

Decisions will also be influenced by the temptation to become and remain a victim. Whatever sort of crisis she endures, a woman must work through the victim syndrome and replace it with the mentality of a survivor. If she feels betrayed by someone she trusted, a victim will be tempted to seek revenge; to inflict as much hurt as she has felt. Any decisions she makes thus will be rooted in bitterness. It seems natural for a woman who loses her health to exclaim the victim's cry, Why me, God? Nor does it diminish the anguish of a woman ending her marriage for a lawyer to cite rising divorce figures. She replies that she is a person, not a percentage. Yet, as long as a woman personalizes whatever tragedy or trouble has befallen her, she will make decisions as a victim rather than as a survivor.

The distinction between the two states of mind is essential. A victim is helpless. She is caught in circumstances that are beyond her control. A survivor is one who goes on—even if only for a few months. She decides much about the way in which she will live, and these decisions enable her to triumph over her troubles somewhat. The terms of this survivorship may not be what she expected or prefers. She may not yet know fully how she will survive the crisis, but she believes that she will. She looks beyond, makes plans accordingly, and rejects the victim syndrome.

A woman has to decide for herself to be a survivor rather than a victim. The choice takes courage and force of mind. It is far easier to remain a sufferer, an object of pity. Pain, mistakes, or defeat loom so large in a victim's thinking that initiative can be paralyzed. However, even in the worst predicament a person can refuse to be a victim. An individual can gather strength to throw off helplessness or strike out in some new direction. Life always offers more fresh starts than any of us ever has the time or the will to take. Older people testify that living sometimes seems to consist of many deaths followed by many resurrections.

Coming through an ordeal, then, requires new ways of thinking and behaving. Habitual thought patterns and attitudes will not suffice. Any crisis casts an atmosphere of strangeness over everyday life. At the outset a woman may feel that nothing will ever be quite the same again. This sense of differentness will be the means by which she starts seeing possibilities for living on. Even before the worst pain recedes, she can open up and begin considering options. She will be uncomfortable with so much change at once. She may have to resort to uncharacteristic forms of behavior. She finds, surprisingly, that the means to cope with change eventually comes.

Survivors of a crisis learn that life can be renewed even after a devastating loss. They can be thrown into a quandary; maybe paralyzed temporarily. If they have support from family and friends, they come to see that they are never alone. The victim syndrome gradually gives way to a survivor's outlook. Well-chosen expert help may also relieve the burden. A woman who is ill, for example, deliberately tries to select a doctor with whom she can communicate easily. Women in other kinds of crisis situations use community resources to regain a sense of survivorship. The Displaced Homemaker network is one example. Shelters for women who are abused or alcoholics are others.

In a crisis any woman will feel confused and distraught, yet she may be able to hold onto hope. Her hope of renewal comes from God. A person who has lived through a difficult period knows that, strangely, the worst can be survived. In his second letter to the church at Corinth Paul reminded Christians there of what the power of God could mean in extremity: "We are often troubled, but not crushed; sometimes in doubt, but never in despair; there are many enemies, but we are never without a friend; and though badly hurt at times, we are not destroyed" (2 Cor. 4:8–9, Today's English Version).

A shock, bringing sudden recognition of one's vulnerability, can sometimes have an effect on decision making as drastic as that of a crisis. When Lib was widowed, she learned that pension payments from her husband's company would stop. Like countless other employees of his generation, Lib's husband had chosen at retirement to receive larger benefits and relinquish payments to his spouse if she survived him. This decision was made without Lib's knowledge. Loss of the pension check forced Lib to alter her financial assumptions drastically at a time when she was grieving over her husband's sudden death. Lib managed to stay in her home, but she could no longer feel secure financially for old age.

This realization impelled Lib to try to do something not only for herself but also on behalf of countless other women whose plight was worse than her own. She had felt untouched by the recent feminist movement. After all, older women were not the focus of actions for women's rights. However, her population group is growing in numbers and in consciousness. When older women like Lib suddenly gain a sense of how vulnerable they are in contemporary society, they want to fight sexism and age discrimination publicly as well as support one another in private. These women may not have thought they related to the females who marched, picketed, or refused to make coffee at the office twenty years ago when feminism was reborn, yet their awareness links them to earlier activists. This underlying consciousness is the single unifying force among women of all ages today.

Because of Lib's shocking recognition, she began checking into the status of widows like herself, discovering a cluster of problems. She found that, as the nation evolves into an older society, many citizens will never have adequate income. The aging of America is a demographic reality that has enormous implications for women. Females will make up a growing majority of senior citizens, and the poverty rate for them is twice that for older men. Lib learned that in 1980, according to the Census Bureau, single women over sixty-five had a median income of only $4,226, a figure dangerously close to the poverty level for a single person during that year. She was in a population category whose financial status was sinking while their numbers grew. Even when the U.S. birth rate declined recently, the mortality rate also declined. Average life expectancy at birth had extended from forty-seven years in 1900 to seventy-four years by 1981.

Lib began to read about a phenomenon labeled "the feminization of poverty." Her personal financial setback was dwarfed by the complexities of this problem. While women live longer than men, they earn significantly less. Older women who were lifelong homemakers were never compensated for their work. It is an occupation that falls outside the jobs covered by the Social Security system. The only support that retired homemakers can claim from this system comes in dependents' benefits. Social Security was never intended to provide full support, but nearly two-thirds of America's older women rely on this source of income alone. Lib now understood why the poverty rate was serious for women in her age group. She also recognized that, while reformers deplore the exclusion of homemakers from Social Security per se, the foundering system was not likely to assume a group of countless new beneficiaries.

At this point Lib still felt moved to take action but overwhelmed by the prospect of trying to change big government. Could alarmed citizens like herself match the effectiveness of skilled lobbyists in the corridors of Congress? Would women simply have to hope they could raise the level of their own earnings in order to remove the shadow of old-age insecurity? Two facts kept her active in the cause of financial security for older women. One was learning that a new law had corrected the practice of employees waiving pension coverage for their survivors without their consent. Along with other improvements in pension benefits for women, the legislation prevented a spouse from doing what Lib's husband had done. Other reforms could follow. Second, she came to appreciate that, while women are undeniably vulnerable, they are the majority in a nation where numbers convert to political power. Lib was still a novice about political pressure and congressional votes, but she saw women's potential to effect change. Her shock eventually led to effective action.

Other less dramatic conditions can call for choices, changes, or making a fresh start. One is a vague, nagging sense of misery that builds to cloud over everyday life. A quality of flatness inheres in everything. A woman in this state finds less and less satisfaction with the status quo. She feels unfulfilled. Second, she may experience flashes of insight, painful but fleeting moments. If these moments lasted longer, they would make life unbearable. Before the sufferer can understand why things seem not at all what they ought to be, however, the feeling disappears. A third circumstance that prompts decision making is a milestone or a major transition. A woman may perceive this as a time to take action or resolve a dilemma. If she is conscious of their significance, a woman can transform these conditions into important turning points in her life.

A miserable person may need the encouragement of friends to initiate a change that will make life more satisfying. Women can struggle silently with misery for a very long time. Many blame themselves for lack of fulfillment. If they remain withdrawn, they may continue to believe the unhappiness is their own fault. Women may go so far as to discuss changes or new directions with someone, yet they may hold back from taking action. One individual may doubt that she can justify asking her family to make adjustments in order for her to explore an option. Another tells herself she should be ashamed for feeling unhappy when she is really a lucky woman. She rationalizes avoiding action by saying to herself that things could be worse.

If a woman gets into such binds, good friends could encourage her to start to move. Friends can interpret her misery as legitimate evidence that she should change; should enlarge her life. Any organism that is alive eventually reacts to pain. If the misery becomes great enough or persists long enough, an individual eventually will do something about the problem. Yet the path to a more satisfying future could be shorter if friends are there to tell her to pick up the phone, make a contact, try something new.

Longstanding friendships can benefit a misery-laden person in several ways. When friends know one another well and accept each other, that knowledge affords perspective to the decision maker. She is reminded of her strengths and unique traits. A friend can hold out hope when the decision maker believes she has lost it. Sometimes a friend simply gets her to laugh—especially at herself.

Nothing helps break anxiety's grip like a humorous moment. A friend who shares life's ups and downs can help one to keep the problems in proportion to the blessings of life. The strongest friendships rest on honesty and confidentiality. A woman can say exactly what is on her mind to a real friend, knowing the revelation will go no farther. Sometimes a friend will push a person about a decision when she is least expecting to be prodded. She may call that encouragement mere luck or accidental. However, a woman looking back over her life with faith's vision can sometimes see that God provided the blessing of a friend when it was most needed.

In addition to deep-felt misery, a woman becomes aware of the need to change through momentary insights. Most people shrug off these odd moments when they shiver and wonder, "Is this all?" Women attribute it to a touch of the blues and plan something enjoyable to shake off the sad thought. Sometimes these fleeting moments bring a sinking sensation. "I missed something important back there somewhere." This impression can even balloon into a kind of fantasy. "There's been a cosmic goof. I'm in the wrong life. I was supposed to be a renowned opera singer, a saintly medical missionary, a distinguished public official." More often, however, the person dismisses the possibility of living the wrong life and throws herself back into the one she's got.

A woman who is busy and knows she is needed can easily put down her moments of insight in straightforward fashion and get on with her work. When tempted to wonder whether life should not offer more than this, she might react with fatalism. "Nobody can really change her life once it's all set." Besides, every day holds so many tasks that the odd fluttering may be ignored. It seems enough to meet one's responsibilities, to keep the routine going. The insight could be a signal almost too faint to be heard over the busyness. If a woman listens to that signal, however, she may learn a great deal about herself.

Some women try to ignore insightful moments by blaming others for an unsatisfactory status quo. Sometimes it is the employer who has forced her into a pigeonhole. "I'm under so much pressure at the firm," one woman complained. "I reached my limit with this company long before I realized it. Those below me are watching for any sign of slackness. They'll run over me if they get the chance. Yet, with the economy so soft, who in her right mind would try to make a change? I'm locked in." Another commented, "Day or night I keep getting the strangest thoughts, but I'm not about to have an identity crisis. Who would do that pile of laundry, help the kids with their homework, deliver the mobile meals? I can't see that I have a choice. That's the way it is."

What happens when a woman starts paying attention to her fleeting insights? Even if she is willing to believe that these are important signals, they seem elusive. A flash of lightning illuminates the night to a remarkable degree, but it will not give light to travel by. How can she turn these promptings into self-knowledge and wisdom? To begin with, she can ponder that the stirrings may actually be moments of truth. In the ancient world one meaning of time was expressed in the Greek word, *kairos*. It was when something important came to pass or when the time was ripe for fulfillment. In the Hellenic view, certain times held unique significance for the individual with vision.

Likewise, in contemporary life, time has an unusual quality when something important is at stake. Those who are open to the possibility of change or who are reaching out for a fuller life may experience *kairos* today. The stirrings or signals could prove to be kairotic moments, precursors to a decisive, insightful period in one's life. A woman could decide that she has been marking time, letting a precious gift slip through her fingers. This insight could lead to a new vision of her remaining time. It may not be too strong to say that adopting a new attitude toward time could be the key to changing one's life.

Besides misery and insight, a milestone or major transition can set the stage for decision making. These occasions are harder to ignore than blue periods or moments of truth. They sometimes give rise to quite painful or poignant feelings. Whether the milestone is retirement, a noteworthy birthday, or some other life change, it can trigger questions that a woman wants to answer. Otherwise, she may be unable to affirm the time already lived or anticipate the future. A young woman about to graduate from high school or college dreamed of doing so many things while preparing for life.

Now she views the tiny slot she will actually occupy and feels unbearable loss. The fact that she never stood much chance of instant fame or greatness is little consolation. She needs to shed childish illusions and grab hold of real hope.

In middle age all people sense that the course of life is narrowing, but women face a special milestone. They cross the biological Rubicon when they experience menopause. Research currently underway is making it possible to understand this complex phenomenon better and help women handle both the psychological and physiological symptoms. Some are surprised by the intensity of their reaction. "For years I was never particularly concerned about my womanness," remarked one, "and was a believer in mind over matter. When things got rough, however, I joined a support group rather than taking hormones. I've never regretted the choice."

At a transition time one may be haunted by the fear of wasted time. When notice arrives of a high school or college reunion, a woman can scarcely believe that so many years have passed. "Where has the time gone?" she wonders. "In some ways it seems so short. I've kept busy every day. But why haven't I done more in a quarter of a century?" She may conclude that she has been kept so busy doing things she *has* to do that she never found time to do those things she really *wanted* to do. Retirement is another milestone that can bring double pressure to a married female worker. She may feel disappointed with her own meager career record but compelled to help her husband adjust as well. If she suffers recriminations over dashed ambitions and her husband is unprepared for his dislocation from the office, their home could become hostile territory. Retirement can trigger a haunting sense of having little time left.

Decision making is often prompted by a desire to use time more wisely. No one wants to look back on decades mainly with regret. A milestone or even a sad time may produce only unspecific feelings. "Nothing really terrible has happened," admitted one woman, "I've simply ended up somewhere I never intended to be. I can't pretend I'm happy, but I am not sure what would satisfy me now." More often, however, the emotion connects to a goal, an ambition, or a resumption of earlier plans. Inwardly she tells herself, "I've got to try this before it's too late." If she accepts the "wisdom of the unconscious," she will realize that it is time to make some plans. Many promising decisions are probably aborted because a person assumes it is "too late." The cultural bias toward youth tricks many Americans into thinking that they have passed the point of being able to make a fresh start or try a new interest or take a different job.

This false notion that it is "too late" can rob a person of fulfillment. Women who have reached the age of sixty still have, on average, more than twenty-two years to live. In her book, *Women and Anxiety*, Dr. Helen DeRosis suggests that women use time in their favor rather than viewing it as an enemy. She urges women to initiate a slight change for the better in their lives during a year. If encouraged by the improvement, they can keep at it and try another change. "Just think," Dr. DeRosis writes, "how all those *small* increments in growth will add up after five years—after ten years."[1] Perhaps this technique will help a woman who would like to believe that it is not "too late" for her to live more fully.

Eventually, whether through crisis, dissatisfaction, or having arrived at some milestone, she considers change. Recognition of the need to change brings an individual to the threshold of decision making. How does she go about it? In his book, *How People Change*, psychiatrist Allen Wheelis gives a moving account of a person faced with the need to change. Rather than discussing a patient's case, Wheelis reveals a bit about himself. He relives a painful childhood confrontation with his dying father. The harrowing experience became a powerful determining force in the doctor's adult behavior. Wheelis decided to struggle with the effect this memory was having upon his life.

The resulting volume is a fascinating consideration of a person's potential for change. Although the psychiatrist emphasizes how limited change often proves to be, he identifies the crux of the process. In order to change, a person must first understand how she came to be what she is. Self-knowledge (already described as a lifelong task) springs a woman loose from the past to begin changing. Second, she must apprehend that a power to choose lies within her. Once she has come to terms with her personal past, she can choose to be different from what she was. She can decide about her future. Why is the possibility for change often not activated? Probably because anyone who has thought about the process very much realizes that it will be hard. Possibly she thinks the change would require more strength than she could muster. Wheelis confirms the suspicion. "The sequence," he writes, "is suffering, insight, will, action, change. The one who suffers, who wants to change, must bear responsibility all the way."[2]

The alibis for not changing appear at any age. "Just look at me," an exasperated forty-three-year-old exclaimed. "I'm up to my eyeballs in kids, housework, and a Type-A husband who's driven to be an executive vice-president. It's all I can do to hold this volatile mix together. And you're telling me to create a self?" A younger woman thought it was unreasonable on different grounds. "Some women can go chasing after rainbows if they like, but I'm sticking right here. Sure, I know the guy down the hall gets more than I do for the same job and takes only half the flak I get from the boss or the girls in the typing pool. I went through a lot to get this far, and at least I know what I'm up against."

Ironically, the loudest protests often are voiced when a woman is about to change; to start creating a self. Alibis may be fear or tiredness speaking. Through his book and lectures psychiatrist Scott Peck has illuminated this inner struggle of those wanting to change. He does not slight the force of inertia. Like Allen Wheelis, Peck acknowledges that it is hard work for an individual to live more authentically. He holds out hope, however, that "even if we seem to be totally fearful and completely rigid, there is still a part of us, however small, that wants us to grow, that likes change and development, that is attracted to the new and the unknown, and that is willing to do the work and take the risks involved in spiritual evolution."[3]

It is essential, then, to keep believing in the possibility of change; to visualize the future as open rather than predetermined. Through such a vision a woman claims a strong truth: each individual creates her own life. Moreover, the creation process usually starts with recognition of the need to change! At midlife, for instance, a woman decides to change. Impelled by a mixture of panic and regret, she proclaims inwardly, "It's now or never." Facing a narrowing course of time, she recognizes that the alternative to creating a stronger self could be tragic. Suppose she has been wholly dependent on significant others—parents, husband, children—for livelihood in every sense. She decides that in today's society such dependency bears too much risk. Besides, after a period of child rearing, half a lifetime may lie ahead for her with little preparation for those decades.

Rather than continue pouring all of her self into the needs and demands of her significant others, a woman in her middle or later years begins to establish a separate identity. The pattern is not easy to break. One woman reflected, "Since childhood I've liked feeling needed. I know I've taken care of people and managed things that no one else could or would have done. That knowledge gives me satisfaction and real fulfillment. It's been hard for me to realize that I should build another dimension to my life." She chose to add a vocational dimension but volunteerism, political activism, or self-enrichment were equally promising options. Like so many of her generation, she started to develop a self independent of those for whom she cares so deeply.

The decision-making process begins, then, with the isolation of a goal, a choice, a possible change. The steps are undertaken in the hope that they will lead to renewal, a more satisfying or enlarged existence. A woman may not be altogether sure at the outset what her eventual decision will be. As she moves ahead through the process, she may come to recognize that she faces a succession of decisions and a long transitional period. She hesitates initially. She dislikes taking risks. However, she dreads regret even more. The possibility of the future stirs her to try, and from this point, there is no turning back.

If she is willing to believe that life is as full of strange possibilities as limiting circumstances, her understanding will grow to meet unfolding circumstances. Directions will become clearer only as she begins to move, however. She must have experience in order to take each step with more certainty. If a woman is new at making decisions, she may find the need to choose, decide, or change burdensome at first. In time she will come to regard it as a gift. She shares the capacity for reflection and reason with all people. The ability to decide sets *Homo sapiens* apart from other species with whom the planet is shared. So long as she does not attempt too much change at once and works through each step in succession, the decision maker should make progress.

Going a Step Further:

1. Suppose you had only one year to live? Seven days? What would you do with that time?
2. Talk to a woman who has worked effectively in the civic arena to initiate a change or challenge the status quo. After analyzing how she went about taking action, decide what was the key to her success.
3. Write a page about a substantial decision that you should make within the coming year.
4. Discuss with an elderly person how she or he looks back upon past decisions. Is the conversation full of contentment and satisfaction, or does the individual reveal regret about these choices?

5

Step 1 in Decision Making:
ESTABLISH THE GIVENS

A woman begins the decision-making process by establishing the givens. The givens are two-fold: her limits and her priorities. Limits are circumstances that will not change. Priorities are elements that she wants to add in the end as well as those elements she would most regret losing. A decision maker will not proceed very far until she is sure of the givens. To some extent they will structure the process and help define the steps that lie ahead. Acknowledging the limits of existence is generally part of one's growing up. During decision making, however, this phase of Step 1 has a special meaning. It reveals that life's finitude is not a barrier but a strong foundation. If a woman becomes clear about her givens, they can point her toward making choices that are right for her.

While a woman's limits might be construed as almost any condition she could mention about herself, she lists usually only those that will have an impact on the projected decision. An individual is unlikely to review her total situation for every decision, yet it is wise to have this totality in mind. Comfortable familiarity with one's overall limits is preferable to gaps in understanding or, worse yet, blind spots about one's self. Here the advantage of keeping a lifeline or up-to-date autobiography comes in. Even when the person concentrates on those elements that pertain to the choice under consideration, the list of limits may include a variety of items from geography to personality. Any individual lives at a particular moment in human history, endowed with specific genes, and after two decades or so, encumbered with a personal past.

A strongly limiting circumstance may appear in a woman's life very abruptly and precipitate difficult decisions. The cases of Marian and Holly illustrate this reality. Marian is newly widowed at age fifty-two and well aware of the limits which this event has placed on her future. She may never be a married person again. Eighty-five percent of surviving spouses are female. Moreover, older men tend to marry younger women. It might seem that this given destines Marian to a long period of living alone in the house she and her late husband built. Yet this may not be so at all. The husband of the second woman, Holly, suddenly moved out. Now she must decide whether the marriage is viable at all. Like so many other contemporary women, Marian and Holly experienced an unexpected limit when their marital status changed.

Even before the shock wore off, Holly recognized that she would have to initiate decision making rather than continue simply to react to the new given. She will have to force the issue of marital counseling with her estranged husband. She could have to take the initiative in consulting an attorney later. She has heard enough about the legal and financial complications of separation and divorce to begin investigating the laws and regulations of her state. Though at first she believed that the blowup which preceded his packing up was a chance event, she now is coming to accept that this shocking given was deeply rooted in their relationship. "Looking back," Holly said, "I can see that he had moved out on me long ago. The blowup was the occasion he chose to depart physically. I know the reasons he gave are not the real problems."

Joann, another decision maker whose marriage ended, weighed the givens of family history and heredity in her considerations. She and her husband have been divorced for two years. He has consistently lagged behind in child support payments for their three youngsters. Now Joann has received nothing for sixty days. Her ex-husband is presently trying to start his own business and should, in time, make a go of this undertaking. Yet Joann and her children cannot wait for the firm to become successful. The children love their father and would suffer if they lost contact with him altogether. Therefore, up till now Joann has not made a serious issue of his late payments for the sake of harmony and civility.

Other facts from the past enter into Joann's thinking. She knows that her former husband's father abused his family, then ran away and left them. Knowledge of this abandonment troubles her at times. A counselor has explained that the pattern of repeating violence through generations seems well established. Joann understands that a victim of abuse, such as her ex-husband, undergoes a tough decision to seek help and try to break the cycle. Yet she herself comes from a long line of spunky, strong women who triumphed over adversity and setbacks. Knowing this about her background gives Joann strength. It encourages her to stand up for what is right even if it means having a confrontation of some sort. In conversations with other divorced mothers, however, Joann hears that any legal steps she might take will be costly, painful, and may do more harm than good. How can her ex-husband build his business if he is in jail? As Joann reaches the point of taking action, she will factor all of this background information into the choices she weighs.

Counseling helped Joann keep these limits in perspective. She was advised that, besides income problems, divorced persons can expect significant psychological pressures. Research has revealed that the process of divorcing and adjusting to a new situation creates stress surpassed only by the effect of widowhood. Bitter emotions surrounding divorce can even result in illness and disease, according to long-term medical investigations.

The adjustment is usually complicated when children are part of the broken family. Each parent suffers from custody fights. Alimony and child support payments are an unreliable basis for livelihood. The Census Bureau reported recently that fewer than one-half of divorced fathers met child support obligations at all. Payments throughout a year averaged only $1,000 per child. Mediators hope that joint custody and continuing relations between child and parent could improve this pattern. Information such as this could help Joann to decide to delay a serious confrontation at this time.

Genes constitute another major part of anyone's limits. A woman's biological background sometimes figures prominently in her decision making. If she knows that several females in her family have had cancer of the reproductive organs, for instance, she will check her breasts for lumps and have Pap smears faithfully. This given may also influence her choice of treatment for severe symptoms during menopause. Science has moved to dramatic new levels of understanding in the field of genetics recently. Individual women should likewise broaden their knowledge of genetic patterns that might be relevant to their personal decisions.

Body type, general health, energy levels, a tendency to certain diseases or physical problems are all givens in one's background that could become considerations in a decision. A teenager was falling into a pattern that would soon classify as anorexia nervosa. This young woman cannot change the fact that she arrived with a hefty heritage at a social moment when thinness is prized! Much as she would like to deny it, this is a given. Nor can she escape the fact that, in order to attain the figure she idealizes, she could develop long-term health problems. The young woman was more fortunate than many of her generation whose genetic makeup has produced a given which they are not prepared to accept.

The teenager became the patient of a sympathetic but firm physician. Through the doctor's intervention, she was able to face what was happening to her health. She accepted that she was the only one who could really cast off this false vision of her self. She did not wish to become anorectic. Nevertheless, the young woman needed plenty of support while she acquired some self-acceptance. People often wish to make a decision that involves a health-related given, quickly become discouraged, and give up on the change. Effecting a change that would improve one's health calls for strong support from family and sometimes a doctor. Attacking a given in this area also needs to be done in manageable steps.

At times a woman wrestles with a given that stems from a personality problem. By midlife she can know this given all too well. Such an individual related that at age forty-four she had become intensely jealous of her husband's female business associate. This wife had found it difficult to trust men for most of her adult life. She knew her given was rooted in childhood troubles. In this case, she thought her suspicions were groundless, but the resentful feelings were poisoning her mind. She could not undo the upbringing that was at the root of her jealousy. She did not want to bring her feelings of jealousy into the open and talk about them with her husband. By herself, she said, she wanted to attempt to work through the emotions before they ruined her marriage. At this point preserving the integrity of their relationship had priority over anything else in her life.

Aside from personal limitations, to some extent the cultural climate can function as a given when decisions must be made. All people are profoundly affected by the spirit of the times in which they live. Sometimes when a woman is considering an important change, it may help if she reminds herself how strongly she could be influenced by cultural bias. For instance, many women who grew up into the emergence of the new feminism have different attitudes than those who were reared and educated earlier. The present climate of opinion makes it difficult for some to justify being "nothing more" than a housewife. These same women might never have considered "housewife" to be a dirty word thirty years ago. Researchers have detected signs that some women decide to enter the labor force partly because they feel social pressure.

This same cultural milieu has influenced other women's choices negatively. As already emphasized, when one's lifeline coincides with a time of rapid change, the social upheaval can generate significant personal conflict. While significant numbers of women are choosing to move beyond the domestic sphere, a highly vocal segment of the female population is working to reestablish the legitimacy of being simply a housewife. These activists explain that initially they expected the cultural phenomenon to pass away. When the changes grew and new values emerged, they decided to launch a counterattack against feminism. They have resolved the conflict which the new cultural environment produced in their lives by championing values, attitudes, and lifestyles at the opposite end of the social spectrum from feminism. The majority of the female population makes choices and faces everyday reality somewhere in between these polarized activists. Yet their decisions can be affected by the position of both extremes on occasion.

Past decisions may also be limits to future plans and choices. Nancy and her husband revealed how strongly a previous pattern affected a pending decision. They explained that they must soon do something about their grown son who lives at home. Having finally run out of rationalizations and false optimism, Nancy and her husband know it is up to them to break a pattern they helped create. The couple's words reflect the dilemma of countless other parents who were thwarted by adolescence. It was one thing, they said, to care for an infant or handle a child but something quite different to cope with a disobedient, sullen teenager who then grew into a floundering young adult. It would be wonderful if they could go back to their son's ninth grade year when he began to go off track and recapture his lost promise. This is not possible. The young man gives every sign of remaining irresponsible and rebellious. The three members of this family struggle to be honest at last and sadly find a way out of this dilemma born of past actions.

How can individuals like Nancy, her son, and husband plan a future when the consequences of the past weigh on their family so heavily? In addition to sound professional help, they have tried to put the dynamics of commitment to work for them. All three still believe in the validity of their family ties. They know that, in a cultural environment where families frequently move, abruptly split, and are easily disillusioned with one another, commitment is not easily maintained. They must remain determined not to give up easily. They understand more clearly than ever that what happens within the walls of a home can nurture every person or produce alienation. They see that conscious choices will shape a positive or harmful pattern, so they remain close to social institutions that offer support to their family and try to keep things together. The notion of commitment has helped Nancy to recognize that a family can be an entity greater than the individuals comprising it. She hopes to build beyond the limits of previous bad decisions.

When a decision maker reviews her limits, she sometimes gets bogged down in recriminations and confuses these with honesty. When some women are asked to be honest about themselves, they look as if they had been accused of a serious crime. They then proceed to censure themselves to a degree that would pain a medieval ascetic! At the beginning of the chapter we met Holly, whose husband had left. This event produced some recriminations as well as decisions for the woman. Holly found it difficult at first not to blame herself for dropping her career "like a hot brick and devoting myself completely to Bill and the children for years on end." Since her husband rationalized his leaving by accusing Holly of being boring to live with, she kept wondering, "Do you suppose Bill might not have strayed if I'd been an interesting career gal instead of a housewife? And I'd have something else in my life now besides all of this emptiness."

While the right sort of honesty is essential at this stage of decision making, recriminations will not help the process move along. A woman who is trying to make a fresh start or bring about a change in her life must beware of self-abasement. Like Holly, she can dwell endlessly on the shortcomings and spend a lot of time in self-reproach. Such a person can be so hard on herself that she will fail to recognize fresh possibilities that are making their appearance in her life.

How can a woman be honest without sinking into recriminations? Some individuals find that experiencing God as a forgiving force releases them from dwelling on past failures. Though they expect to be judged by God, they find instead a Spirit that takes the initiative in setting them free from the past. Paul reiterated this transforming reality of Christ's work in 2 Corinthians when he wrote, "Now the Lord is the Spirit, and where the Spirit of the Lord is, there is freedom" (2 Cor. 3:17).

It might seem contradictory to introduce the idea of freedom into a discussion of limits, but that is exactly what decision makers should do. Here is a paradox that happens to contain a helpful truth: if a woman will name the limits, the effort will point her toward proper exercise of her limited BUT VERY REAL freedom of action. She will never have to choose among any and all possibilities. Her limits have taken care of that. Once she completes the next phase of Step 1 and decides where her priorities lie, she can devote full energies to the remaining steps. She is then free to bring whatever plan she shapes to pass. Her limits have ceased to be just obstacles that she bumps against but have become a ground of being instead.

Marian, the woman whose sudden widowhood brought a powerful given into her life, struggled to claim the truth of this paradox. Finally she saw that, despite circumstances that won't change, freedom to be a certain kind of person does exist. Early in the grief process Marian assumed that she had only two choices. She could remarry or remain in her house alone. Eventually she reached the point in recovery that she began to think more actively about her future circumstances.

While we will review only the options which Marian considered in the "shelter" area of her life, she found that she had choices in other components as well. Marian began by investigating new possibilities that would not have arisen while her husband was alive. She found that agencies to match potential home-sharers exist in many locations today. Another alternative to remaining alone in her dwelling was to rent part of the house to graduate students at a nearby university.

Marian discovered, like many single older women, that she did have options within her limits. Residential arrangements suited a variety of financial levels. She checked out purchasing a unit in an apartment complex and even joining a communal home. The idea of transferring to a retirement community was one which her children raised. The entire family also discussed whether Marian might want to live with a grown child, perhaps in separate quarters. For the time being Marian chose to retain her present home. Along with increasing numbers of widows, however, she made plans to share her living space with nonrelated "family."

Over a period of time Marian learned that freedom is not just an abstract notion to be read about in books or revered on the Fourth of July. It is a reality that comes alive when people decide and take action. A woman is free because of what she does—not because of circumstances of birth or good luck. Marian will never share her and her husband's dream home with him again. That is a given, however much she wishes it otherwise. Yet she has found the freedom within limits. She is free to live alone or she can, on the other hand, share commonplace pleasures of living with one other, dozens, or even hundreds.

A woman who progresses through such ideas comes, like Marian, to view her limits as a framework within which she can be her unique self. She won't remain stuck, wishing for more talent, fewer problems, different relatives, a better deal. She sees that her being alive at all is a wonder whether she computes mathematically or ponders philosophically. She accepts being born into a certain family with the physical makeup which their genes produced. She lives in a particular place and has done some things which give her a personal past. Her talents or her situation may not be all that she would like them to be. Her accomplishments may not amount to much by contemporary notions of success. Just knowing that she is free to grow, develop, and decide can be a priceless asset, however.

Why is the possibility of freedom within limits so hard to grasp? The pressures of daily living partially obscure this reality for many people. Also some individuals prefer to dwell on life's limitations rather than deal with the unnerving prospect of freedom of action. They feel uncomfortable or burdened by the opportunity to choose. They continue to reassure themselves that their limits have closed off potentiality of change. Others refuse to allow their limits to become primarily a wellspring of regret. The only regret they fear is dying without ever having lived in a way that is authentic and unique. If a decision maker can see the reality of freedom shining through even dark limits and goes ahead to decide what is important to her, then she will feel her life begin to move.

Therefore, the second task which a woman must accomplish at Step 1 is to determine what her priorities are and then rank them. Many decision makers shy away from the process. They complain that it is time-consuming and not easily accomplished. Both reactions are somewhat valid. However, the exercise has offsetting benefits: it can remove one cause of bad decisions and wrong choices, it will cut down on a decision maker's confusion, and, it could prevent her swinging endlessly from one alternative to another. Before she gets too far into planning a change or taking action, a woman should by herself set the relative importance of key elements in her life. Determining one's priorities encourages an individual to think about dimensions she could add to her life and gives her greater appreciation for those she would not wish to lose.

"How do I begin to determine my priorities?" Jean asked during a workshop on decision making. "In the first place they seem always to be shifting, depending on what's happening in my life and even according to the mood I'm in. I couldn't really say what long-term priorities should be for me, much less rank them." Jean's question reflected the state of mind of someone who could use a lifeline to good advantage. It might bring some hitherto unfocused parts of Jean's life clearly before her. After trying an exercise designed to increase self-knowledge, Jean approached the problem of priorities in a very different way. She saw that she did have recurring desires and needed the opportunity to develop these. She began to weigh changes against the probability that they would enhance these valued parts of her life. Some decisions clearly would fit with Jean's emerging list of priorities. Others would not. Most significantly, Jean began to be more willing to trust her own judgment and to accept that she could in fact determine her priorities.

A woman who is at this step of decision making may be tempted to confuse her own priorities with those held by others close to her. She has to state what is significant to her and then communicate these priorities to the others. Women are sometimes at pains to separate their own priorities when the bond with their significant others is very strong, as the example of a young bride reveals. Both the man and woman have jobs, and she is taking evening courses for an MBA as well. She and her husband have mutual respect for one another's abilities and personal ambitions. They also share a hope that they will build a strong, satisfying union. In the months following their wedding, however, she senses that her own routine has changed far more than her husband's has. His unexpected promotion means that he stays at the office longer and longer. She finds herself assuming more of the domestic responsibilities than anticipated.

The bride makes a kind of psychological audit that reaffirms her priorities. She discovers that their relationship is tilting almost imperceptibly but steadily to favor his needs and vocational future over hers. She admits that for the moment she enjoys looking after things at home more than working on her MBA courses. Her husband obviously is happy to have this extra loving support as he learns his new job. Yet she decides it is time to clarify matters by reminding her husband of their promise to balance elements in their marriage. Both know that a family intending to balance the load must work at the task. When demands conflict, negotiations, concessions, and compromise must take place. Each person must be willing to consider the needs of the others. Furthermore, since human relationships are always changing, the balance will have to be adjusted periodically. This bride decided not to allow newlywed euphoria to obscure her professional goals.

A second bride had an experience that pointed up the value of communicating one's priorities openly. She and her new husband tried and tried to agree on a budget. Their effort always foundered. The financial decisions of one seemed to rile the other. Finally the wife revealed a deep desire that was affecting this wrangling over spending. She wanted them somehow to purchase a "starter" home as soon as possible. Her husband had no inkling that she attached so much importance to this financial decision. Up to now the wife had scarcely realized that it was quite so high on her list of priorities. She knew that her husband thought home ownership would be an unwanted burden at this point in their life. Neither, he insisted, had time to spare for upkeep or money to spend on insurance, taxes, or renovation.

Nonetheless, the wife explained her priority fully to her husband. She admitted that she had unconsciously been rejecting any budget that did not aim toward this step and revealed both the psychological and financial reasons behind her priority. Upon investigation, the latter proved to be even more numerous than she had realized. Besides providing housing, the property would be a good tax shelter. The IRS allows mortgage interest and property taxes as deductions. In recent decades real property values have appreciated more than other forms of investment. Thus home ownership served as a hedge against inflation. Moreover, when a residence is sold after the owner reaches age fifty-five, the person may exclude the first $125,000 of gain from taxable income. Seeing that home ownership offered multiple advantages from serving as collateral for other investments to an ultimate tax windfall, the couple reconsidered the husband's assumption that they should continue to rent their lodgings indefinitely.

Sometimes personal relationships improve dramatically when priorities are brought out into the open by a decision maker. A college sophomore was dating a fellow student more and more seriously. Deep inside she knew she would never feel good about herself if she became sexually involved with the man. Their relationship continued to intensify, but he misinterpreted the direction in which it was going. She knew he was getting conflicting signals, but she did not wish to break off the affair. Finally she got the courage to communicate her priorities to him in a straightforward way. She told him that a sexual relationship would only work for her if it was part of an integrated commitment. She wanted an attachment that was passionate yet satisfying in many other ways. The college student was honest with her boyfriend about this priority and could handle the relationship with much less inner conflict.

Occasionally a decision maker's first priorities can complicate her life further rather than lessen personal conflict. It would be unrealistic not to point out that ranking priorities can force painful elimination of certain other options. This possibility compels a decision maker to make sure she knows what is truly important to her. The experience of Ruth illustrates the point emphatically. Ruth's decision concerned personal ties as well as her job. At twenty-six she was upset when the firm notified her of a pending transfer to another state. Ruth put a lot of herself into her job, but she also devoted much time to a wide circle of friends.

Ruth began to weigh priorities. She had to let her employer know her decision quite soon. Still, she reserved enough time to identify the key aspects of the decision and then place them in order of importance to her. In her mid-twenties Ruth knew she was too young to be closing off all of her possibilities by this decision. Yet she was old enough to have accumulated some valuable associations in her life and was not the kind of person who could cast aside these personal and vocational ties easily. The proposed location which the company selected had never held much appeal for her. Now Ruth looked upon the place negatively. She knew that by refusing to transfer, she might find herself forced to seek another position, which was a disagreeable prospect. Business in her city was generally slow just now, and few women were being hired at her level. Yet in the past four years she had established friendships on which she had really depended.

In the end Ruth refused to accept relocation. Her decision was not well received by the company. She was sidetracked immediately and feared that she might soon be unemployed. Ruth had risked her job by opting to stay where she felt at home. She was in the midst of a circle of strong friends of both sexes. She decided that her first priority was this support system, though she faced a long unsettled period. Job prospects were poor, and her friends could supply limited help. Ruth did not regret her commitment, but she recognized how much courage her predicament would require in the coming months.

Similarly, when close personal relationships figure prominently in the priorities, a woman senses how deeply these ties can influence her decisions. A widow considering remarriage talked about the trouble she was having making up her mind. "My three children are young adults, but they've been behaving like small kids since they realized that Hal and I are serious. I don't blame Hal for resenting their attitude toward him. I don't know if they'll ever accept him as my husband. Hal's not a thing like their father, but he and I feel we could make a go of things together."

The woman set to work sorting out conflicting feelings. She had no wish to disrupt the relationship she had with her children but did not want to lose Hal either. After thinking and writing about her decision, she began to see how to set priorities. Another remark she made revealed how female decision makers can feel torn by apparently irreconcilable personal relationships. "I venture to say that if I were a widower in the same situation, I would probably just introduce the prospective bride and let it go at that! If I'd been their father instead of their mother, I might not even have discussed with the children changes in my will that could be brought on by remarriage."

Neither woman was seeking a way around her givens. The limits were real. The widow's children saw Hal as an interloper and were not likely to accept him readily. He wanted to get married soon and could not see waiting until he won over prospective stepchildren. Ruth's firm took the position that the transfer was in her best interest and that of the corporation. She could not ask her employer to forget the idea. Yet, in the face of these conflicts, each woman shunned false restrictions on her freedom. Each was committed to more authentic living and was not afraid to take some risk.

As each of these two women worked to identify what was at stake in her decision and rank the various elements, she made a discovery. Wrestling with her dilemma, she felt a capability growing within. It was that she really had freedom to choose. The very fact that she had come thus far and was now able to look ahead and shape a future gave her confidence. Recognition of this inner freedom was revitalizing. It lifted her spirits and kept her working to understand the givens. She resisted the temptation to give up and kept looking for unseen possibilities.

Finally, an elderly woman related how an unexpected request reminded her that it might be time to shift some longstanding priorities. For years she had emphatically told her children that she would never share their dwellings. It was her conviction that elderly family members could be unwelcome additions to a household. She had observed that, when they became frail and dependent, very old individuals could endure anything from neglect or indignities to outright abuse. She knew cases where elderly people who had no housing of their own grew more and more helpless in ways not easily comprehended by younger, self-reliant folk. Each of her children knew she held very strong feelings about the matter of moving in with them.

All of her assumptions about the future, she continued, had been based on a plan to move into a retirement complex. When the time was right, she served notice on the family that she was selling her home and relocating. Suddenly her youngest daughter began to beg her mother to come live with her family. They had searching conversations over several weeks time. The mother could see that there was a possibility she might become a mediating force at a troubled time for her daughter's family. She had reservations, and yet this strong-minded woman also appreciated what she could mean to her daughter's family. She said that at times a family must draw upon all of its sources of strength for survival, and to some extent she could offer that ingredient. Would she later regret changing priorities and foregoing her plans? As the following chapter will explain, an unanticipated alternative sometimes can be the right choice for a decision maker. Once she establishes what she most wishes to preserve in the outcome of her decision, she feels free to act in a manner consistent with those priorities.

Going a Step Further:

1. Continue thinking about the pending decision which you identified after reading chapter 4. What would you most regret losing in the outcome?
2. Think back about various "givens" that applied in your important decisions. Try to separate those that were genetically or biologically based from those that were rooted in your cultural environment. Were you aware of the givens at the time?
3. Do you have recurring priorities—components of your life which you have always enjoyed and would not wish to live without?
4. What are some possible endings to the story of the widow considering remarriage to a man whom her children refused to accept?

6

Step 2 in Decision Making:
IDENTIFY
THE ALTERNATIVES

Any situation that calls for a decision or a change requires choosing among alternatives. The individual faced with deciding may think she has merely to choose between two clearcut options. Having already determined her priorities, the person may think the choices are obvious. Creativity is an important part of the process, however. Before taking action she should learn about options that were hitherto unknown. If time permits and her imagination is working, she may devise a far better plan of action. The main thrust of this chapter, therefore, will be to learn how to avoid overlooking any alternative that could result in a better decision. We will concentrate on a person's getting outside help through expert advice and signals from within.

By casting about for previously unconsidered ideas or carefully exploring new avenues, women are pleasantly surprised at what they are able to arrange. They may find a way to combine the best elements of two choices which once seemed to rule one another out. They could stumble onto an unknown but very appealing course of action. Even the most knowledgeable person has gaps in her learning. By giving herself time to investigate and staying open to new ideas, a woman may find herself—at the end of this second step—farther down the road to her goal than she dreamed possible. Decision makers often report that the best alternative was not even on the list initially.

The principal means of enlarging one's thinking and adding to a list of options is through expert advice. Ours is a society of specialists. Almost every occupation boasts of experts who have impressive credentials to boot. As life becomes more complex, people have to call upon outside helpers for information and advice. A woman today can readily gain direct access to expert help wherever she lives by picking up the phone and making an appointment with someone who has expertise in the area of her dilemma. Or she may gain information indirectly through books and community workshops.

The following case illustrates how a woman can seek expert advice at minimum expense in order to discover alternatives of which she was unaware. The story also indicates that a person willing to seek out information can often help many others besides herself. Wanda and three fellow workers suspected that a new processing technique begun at their plant might be exposing those on the line to a toxic substance. They questioned the foreman of their shift who said their fears were groundless. The company would never risk using a process that was both dangerous and illegal. Besides this reassurance, they got a reminder from him that troublemakers in the plant were not looked upon favorably by management. The others decided to drop the matter rather than have to seek another job.

Wanda felt she had to do something about the situation but did not know where to turn. Her husband thought she was making too much of the matter but said he would not try to talk her out of acting. She grew more and more anxious about the dilemma. They counted on her paycheck, and the factory was convenient to their home, yet she just knew she could not turn away from a risk. Should she speak up and get fired or keep silent and be poisoned? Wanda grew almost sick with worry. Finally she shared her concerns with the young minister at their church and explained the bind she was in.

This contact was the first of several conferences that gave Wanda new insight into her problem. The minister referred her to a local legal aid clinic where she met with an attorney who had experience in the field of worker rights. Wanda learned from the lawyer exactly what federal law required under the Occupational Safety and Health Act of 1970. She discovered that the enforcing agency's procedures might help her pressure the company to eliminate a health hazard. She was advised how best to avoid retaliation against her. Armed with legal information about their rights and the support of a lawyer, Wanda approached other employees again. This time she gathered support for making a concerted complaint within the OSHA regulations and under the auspices of the National Labor Relations Board. In a few weeks Wanda progressed from panic to effective action. She had thought just two options were open to her. Being willing to seek outside advice and information, she benefited many besides her own family.

Selecting the best expert should never be a shot in the dark. A woman who suspects that she has a medical problem, for instance, will want to choose a physician on grounds other than hearsay. If a friend does see this doctor, the recommendation may be helpful but only when confirmed by others and reinforced by outside information. Any specialist's background and training can easily be checked out. Reference librarians can show an inquirer various professional directories which explain qualifications in considerable detail. Suppose it becomes necessary to retain the services of an attorney? Blind selection by scanning lawyers' names in the yellow pages could have grievous results. The volumes of *Martindale-Hubbell Law Directory* are one example of a resource that gives background and ratings for members of the legal profession.

Once a woman has made her selection, an appointment with the expert is likely to be more fruitful if she prepares for the conference and arrives armed with a list of relevant questions. Why is this preliminary work so important? If the expert is good, then this specialist is likely to be busy and, possibly, expensive. The initial appointment will involve money and perhaps some awkwardness. If a woman sees an expert prematurely, she may never be sure that the conference was necessary or know how to weigh the advice she receives. She could even leave with a sense of being told everything but what she needed to know and feel more confused about her decision than ever.

A good strategy is to assemble a list of questions and have the paper in plain view during the appointment. Working from written questions is no guarantee that one will receive all the answers on the spot, but it does afford the decision maker some advantages. First, the evidence that the inquirer has done investigating in advance should impress the expert that she is serious and may encourage the specialist to be more informative. Moreover, written questions definitely can prolong a conference. Anyone who has been left in midsentence talking to a departing doctor's flying white coattails or stammered while an IRS bureaucrat eyed his jangling phone knows she might need this bit of leverage to keep the expert talking a little longer.

Therefore the most desirable course of action is to read first and ask questions later. While the number of experts has boomed, "self-help" publications have grown even more. Stop in a library or a bookstore and look at how exhaustively anyone's questions or problems have been analyzed in print. Much of this proliferation is directed at a female readership. Publications treat female health concerns, for example, ranging from overviews in the holistic style to exhaustive explanations of a single illness. Persons needing financial plans or coping with taxes learn about everything from cash flow to W–2 forms. Women can find material that will explain their questions at almost any level of comprehension.

If she is not too pressed for time, a woman can utilize community resources before going to a specific expert. A workshop, seminar, or forum open to the public may address the very concern she has. Financial matters and health problems are as popular in this medium as they are with publishers. One should check with a variety of sponsoring organizations. Religious groups or family life councils hold special programs. The YWCA and continuing education office of a local college offer short courses of general interest. Teenagers can take advantage of career days or college fairs held in many communities. Sometimes these workshops and programs clarify a problem. A couple with financial difficulties may discover that they need counseling about communication as well as information about credit and bankruptcy. Many people use the information gleaned from such public programs as background for a follow-up visit with an individual consultant.

All such preparation could help a woman get off on the right foot with the expert. She can tell a great deal usually from the first appointment. Is the expert willing to be sounded out before establishing a definite patient or client relationship? Does the expert think it worthwhile for the woman to know her/his background and understand the outlook governing the treatment or advice? Does the expert seem interested in their communicating easily and openly? Some experts consider it a drawback to have clients or patients with ideas of their own and do not wish to have someone "second-guess" them. Others are tolerant of give-and-take. Any competent, experienced expert should have his/her professional judgment respected, but this does not rule out consideration of the client or patient.

Even if the expert appears to be approachable, the decision maker must never forget that theirs is a business association. Whether the expert is a realtor, attorney, insurance agent, or marital counselor, the consultant stands to gain financially from their conferences. One hopes this is not the prime consideration, but it will be a factor nonetheless. Therefore a woman wants to get her money's worth. She should have enough background on the matter to know if the advice is inappropriate to her problem or not likely to help much. She may have to decide whether she wants to spend more money on further consultation. The expert may wish to undertake an exhaustive analysis or extensive examination as a first step. Is this a wise commitment of money and effort, especially since it may obligate her to continue as a client or patient?

A woman must always be sufficiently well informed to assess the advice she receives from a specialist. The point cannot be made strongly enough. At the outset she may feel tempted to place herself completely in a professional's hands whether that individual is an accountant, physician, or banker. It could be a struggle to remain skeptical and hardheaded. Yet her security rests on her own judg-ment. Under no circumstances can she depend on experts fully. At the very least, she will have to be competent enough to evaluate ex-pert advice. The recommendations may not be in her own best in-terest. Space does not permit detailed accounts of what has happened to women who forgot or ignored this reality. The results were anything from wasted fees to squandered inheritances. Often genuine tragedy occurred. No decision maker wishes to become the victim of an expert's bad judgment, mismanagement, or outright thievery.

Taking care, a woman can use expert advice to increase and clarify the alternatives. Once she thinks she has located a well-qualified individual, she gathers information on her own. By read-ing only one book before they consult, she could gain a sense of the scope of her decision. She will identify the sort of questions she should ask the expert at this point. If the person strongly recom-mends an immediate course of action, she can better respond to this pressuring advice. She may see the wisdom of the suggestions. At the least, though, she will probably want to take the recommenda-tion under advisement before proceeding. In the long run she will have a better relationship with the person she has consulted if she is questioning, open-minded, and even assertive at first.

It is best to get the input of an expert early in the decision-mak-ing process. As the experience of a woman named Sally shows, early involvement of an expert may increase a woman's list of alter-natives significantly. During a routine check the company nurse found that Sally's blood pressure was quite elevated. Sally went to see her family doctor who told her she should begin taking medica-tion for hypertension. She agreed. The pharmacist who filled her prescription happened to be a friend. He cautioned Sally about the drug's side effects and also revealed that she could expect to be re-filling the order for the rest of her life.

Sally felt torn. She was afraid to ignore the doctor's orders but was bothered by the pharmacist's revelations. A telephone check with the physician brought new insistence that she start the medi-cine and displeasure at having a medical opinion questioned. Sally decided to consult a second doctor about her condition. This time she saw a specialist. The new doctor also happened to be a female. Sally was struck by the contrast in the way her problem was handled by the woman physician. She had not previously been aware that bias against female patients can be a complicating factor in women's health care generally.

When she knew the doctor better, Sally raised the matter and recounted her difficulty in getting her old family physician to discuss treatment alternatives. The specialist mentioned that a recent study by the American Medical Association confirmed what Sally and countless other women experienced. Among married couples who saw the same doctor, the research showed, a husband's symptoms received more serious consideration than the same symptoms on the wife's part. Since over 90 percent of physicians are males, the study would seem to reveal underlying sexism in their approach to patients. Moreover, some afflictions that often prompt a woman to visit her doctor are not those which receive prestigious research efforts with a corresponding status in the medical community. Premenstrual syndrome, menopause, and osteoporosis are examples of these problems. They also have symptoms that a physician may associate with hypochondria or attribute to emotional causes.

Sally's new doctor pieced together a lengthy family history and examined her completely. Then she explained carefully why Sally was a likely candidate for high blood pressure. A definite diagnosis would await a long period of monitoring and measurement, however. Once the doctor established that Sally did have borderline hypertension, the two considered options for treatment. These included a nondrug approach that was promising. Sally learned that, if she wanted to avoid a lifetime of medication she would have to alter some habits. She made a decision that the behavior modification was worth trying. If Sally had simply allowed her problem to go untreated when she left the family doctor, the most desirable alternative might have been closed to her later. As it was, Sally was able to reconcile her desire to take a minimum of powerful, expensive drugs with the doctor's intention to reduce a risk of stroke. Sally was justifiably proud of the outcome of her decision making.

Often the task of identifying the alternatives is an unpleasant process that a woman would rather ignore. No other situation illustrates this fact better than the decisions that follow a death in one's family. A widow, for instance, inevitably must make choices and take actions. How different that experience will be for a woman who investigates options with her spouse early in their marriage than it will be for the individual who never planned. Death is inevitable, and it is far preferable to learn beforehand how to make the decisions that will ensue. If a woman knows what to expect—legally and financially—when a spouse dies, she could alleviate some of the suffering. It is enough to overcome the grief of this personal loss without the added burden of financial devastation. Estate planning is not just for wealthy folks. Anyone who values her own existence and the well-being of her family should formulate plans that are based on good information and keep those plans up-to-date.

It takes real determination to undertake estate planning and become familiar with the steps to be taken at the time of death. Contemporary culture has an undercurrent that wishes to deny death. Whereas our forebears got all too frequent reminders of this painful certainty, it is possible today to avoid confronting it. We can think of many people who pretend that life will just go along endlessly. Cultural preoccupations with routine, trivial matters make it hard to contemplate shattering eventualities. Some courage is required when considering alternatives that are not at all appealing and probably are frightening. Nevertheless, everyone should know what actions will follow at the bank, the Social Security office, and possibly, in probate court. More significantly, a woman should shape plans to insure her future and that of those she loves. These imperatives rest not on morbidity, but on sound legal, psychological, and financial grounds.

Whether she is young or old, a widow must be prepared to take steps that sometimes are complicated. Circumstances differ. Laws are always changing and vary from state to state. However, a woman who has reviewed the most common transactions facing a new widow will not be altogether shocked by what she may be called upon to accomplish. A review will also alert her to the fact that she will require funds to pay some extraordinary expenses. These include medical and burial charges as well as the cost of settling her spouse's estate. The latter expenses consist of various federal and state taxes plus fees to those involved in estate settlement. For instance, an attorney could process the will; an appraiser may assess the deceased person's property; an executor will settle the estate, including payment of his outstanding debts. Liquid assets will be needed from the start.

A widow must think of her spouse's estate in several different ways. One is the probate estate. Generally this consists of all assets which will be transferred to beneficiaries through a will. Property that is jointly held with survivor's rights does not go through probate, for example. If the spouse died without a valid will (i.e., intestate), then the court will appoint an administrator to manage details of estate settlement. Besides the probate estate, the widow must recognize that there is a gross estate for tax purposes. This could be much larger than the probate estate since it includes everything that he owned, wholly or in part. After paying taxes, fees, and debts, the heirs receive the net estate.

Thus a widow acquires an aggregate of resources that she will invest and use to maintain her household along with any earnings of her own. Her assets might include such moneys as the proceeds from the husband's life insurance policies. Other funds could come from his employer. Perhaps these would be from credit union funds and the company pension plan. As already noted, counting on pension benefits could prove to be a false expectation. Holdings such as stocks, bonds, real property, and IRAs eventually will pass to the widow as well as, perhaps, benefits from the Veterans Administration. She will also receive assets in any joint checking and savings accounts. However, these will be frozen, in part, for a time after death.

Additionally, the widow takes steps to arrange for all Social Security benefits to which she and her children are entitled. Social Security payments definitely should not be viewed as an adequate basis for living, though they are, in fact, all the assets that many widows possess. Families receive initially a lump sum death benefit of $255. A widow without children receives no benefits until she reaches age sixty or becomes disabled. Benefits will come to a worker's children until age eighteen or graduation from high school. Note the "widow's gap" which could open up if a woman had children and then lost her husband while she was relatively young! Benefits to the family are computed on the husband's past earnings. The government announced that, in 1983, a surviving family of three only received a maximum of $1,393 per month.

When considering their alternatives in estate planning, a couple aims insofar as possible to keep the family in its accustomed setting. This goal entails careful financial management and a comprehensive plan. When a husband/father is removed from a household by death or divorce, family income usually falls drastically. However, expenses do not decline much and may even rise. For instance, if the widow goes to work, she may bear new child care costs. The government estimates that, *in addition to* funds guaranteeing housing and education of children, a widow will need income totaling 70 percent of her husband's gross annual income to maintain customary lifestyle. Private research indicates that this estimate may be low. Thus, the projected resources required by survivors of a breadwinner who earns $25,000 could be ten times his salary in order for his family to remain in their world following his death. Otherwise, his survivors may not be able to keep their house or carry out college or vocational plans for children.

During the time when a decision maker is trying to identify all of her alternatives, she searches deep within as well as seeking outside advice. Any woman who finds herself in a situation that demands choosing wisely will want to reflect about what she knows lies deep inside. Attentive to inner signals, she may focus on some promising choice that was not conspicuous at first.

She will attach special importance to the practice of silence, particularly if the period is one of pressure, confusion, even unhappiness. Her senses may suffer a greater than normal bombardment. As her external environment grows more hectic, the practice of silence can help. She pushes away some vexations and complications and becomes more mindful of the essentials that are at stake. Times of quiet reflection help maintain balance and perspective. A woman who is wrestling with unresolved dilemmas or managing a transition learns to rely on the practice of silence. If she reflects with expectancy, she could be strengthened and may move closer to deciding.

She might also discover that the element of choice is greater than it first appeared. For example, a woman who wants or needs to reenter the work force today after years at home is daunted by what she learns about the process. The obstacles seem shocking. Older women comprise the fastest growing group of employees in this country. Many of these workers never anticipated being employed. They are often relegated to low level jobs that offer small pay increases while the women work and are an inadequate basis for retirement benefits. Not surprisingly, reentry women dread the prospect of being trapped in a discouraging, demeaning situation. Nonetheless, they may feel initially that they will have to accept "almost anything" in the way of a job.

Rather than take a shortcut that will shortchange her, a woman can draw upon inner resources to resist panic and start searching steadily for the best solution. Job opportunities are far from ideal for many women. Some are in a financial or geographical strait jacket and do not have the luxury of wide exploration. Nevertheless, even within limits, some options offer more joy, honesty, and freedom than others. Reflecting upon what she knows to be her unique qualities, a reentering worker will explore alternatives that encourage her authentic self to develop further.

It may be possible to obtain fresh training or even a diploma before accepting a job. Educational institutions welcome older women as their student populations shrink in the decades following the baby boom. Such nontraditional students often develop strong study skills partly because of limited time and outside responsibilities. Instructors relish their high level of motivation. In the end, college placement offices can be as helpful in the job searches of older graduates as they are to those who are twenty-two.

A woman who is attuned to inner qualities often can better assess the help provided by career counselors or employment agencies. If she has a clear understanding of her best self, then their testing or leads can be measured against that self-knowledge. Career counseling is presently available at all sorts of community agencies and institutions. Often the assistance comes at a minimum of expense. Most state employment offices have expanded the free services they offer citizens to include testing, counseling, and résumé writing. Some commercial employment agencies specialize in placing women workers. Yet keep in mind that professional advice always means more to someone who has thought privately about aptitudes and interests.

Moreover, inner resources and reflection help an older job seeker cope with the negative feelings that our cultural bias toward youth engenders. Middle-aged women can find that a job search is a desolating experience. Both societal emphasis on youth and economic pressures would seem to favor younger applicants over those who are mature. An older person can easily come to think that her age is a greater disadvantage than it is. She may overlook the fact that there are special niches in the workplace where older employees are valued for their stability, their people skills, and above all, their determination. A job search is tough at any age. Individuals in midlife and beyond often have a resiliency born of experiencing ups and downs that younger adults have yet to acquire.

Finally, it will probably be strength from within rather than outside encouragement that enables a job seeker to make the extra, hard effort that results in both salary and satisfaction. A reentry woman may fear that any more time spent in searching will not be productive. The fact that she has to keep paying for her necessities adds pressure to make a quick decision. If she receives an early offer through a personal contact, she may want to snatch it up and cast aside larger ambitions. Already somewhat resentful at starting over, she might just take her first offer and end the quest. On the other hand, she could find the inner resolve to search a little longer. Knowing that eight hours of every working day is a long time to be miserable, she keeps other factors in view besides buying groceries and paying rent. She may locate a work environment that promotes the intangibles which she prizes.

Any decision maker can anticipate God's guidance as she investigates and identifies various alternatives. Moving toward making a decision, she might want to review a teaching of Jesus that is relevant to the process. Recorded both in Matthew 7:7–11 and Luke 11:5–13, the teaching seems to emphasize that God helps those who are willing to take action in their own behalf. In no case, Jesus seems to say, should one simply ask God for help, then wait passively for the request to be fulfilled. The version in Luke stresses the need for persistent effort even more strongly than that in Matthew. Some commentators suggest that the person needing bread from a sleeping friend at midnight got the food, not simply because of their friendship but because he persisted.

The promised help may come in surprising ways. Struggling to make the right decision, a woman may unaccountably feel strength she did not think she possessed. Suddenly she will seem bolstered in her efforts and gain fresh patience to locate the alternative that will enrich her life. Others, who tend to be hard on themselves when facing choices, may find they are more open to the possibility of joy. They start to ask, "Where is an alternative that will bring greater joy to daily living? Will one choice strengthen hope more than another?" God desires joy and strength in the lives of all people. The Spirit of God helps both these qualities to flourish in one who seeks answers in the light of her own clear needs and within a framework of faith.

As she works at her decision, a woman finds that God's help often comes through caring persons. Time and again individuals look back on a troubled spell and report that this was so. Women trying to decide need to share their concerns with those who know them well just as they must sometimes seek professional advice. A friend or family member may be able to point out some alternative which the bewildered individual has overlooked. Perhaps they will see some good combination of choices which she was too distracted to notice. They can help her assess the advice of experts. Often such persons will encourage her to try something which she lacks confidence to attempt but which may foster her best self. More than one mother has struck off in a new direction at the urging of her children! Although it is the woman herself who must act, the support of offspring can be decisive. Her faith informs her that God is present in the help and advice coming from those who care about her.

Conversely, a woman would do well to avoid distressful persons or situations while she is developing alternatives. She might recognize, for example, that large family gatherings can add to the pressure she feels as easily as they could encourage her. If the occasion is likely to produce negative feelings or increase her anxiety, she should pass it up. She may also decide to withdraw temporarily from some group that would be hard to face at this time. If she is receiving professional help from a counselor, she may discuss the possibility of altering social routines or cutting some ties that could impede the progress she is making. Often the need to separate is obvious without expert advice. A teenager who is uncomfortable with the values of her crowd must stop going out with these friends until she decides what sort of social behavior she can handle. A young couple wishing to reverse overspending patterns will have to swap expensive leisure activities for simpler pleasures.

An individual may have to search more widely than she expected to gather alternatives. The process could take longer than she imagined it would. At fourteen Tanya found herself in conflict with her recently remarried mother and new stepfather. The girl initially thought the best—indeed, the only—choice she had was to run away and find her father. She believed the two adults here saw her as unpaid labor and cared only for themselves. She was not willing to wait around for attention and refused to be hassled about her laziness.

She was crushed to learn that her father was uninterested in his teenage daughter. He promptly sent her back to her mother. With help the girl communicated her feelings to her mother and began a long, uneven process of reconciliation. Tanya, her mother, and her stepfather will not have an easy time together, but they are communicating. Counselors attempted to apply the concept of balancing every family member's needs to their situation.

Parents, especially single parents, may recognize that a child's situation is not ideal. It is estimated that only 38 percent of all American youth now reside with both natural parents. The concept of balancing may help a single parent facing choices that involve a miserable child. For example, by 1990, researchers say, fourteen million American children will be in day child care. The needs of these children will have to be weighed carefully in an equation that is economic, social, and personal. The concept of balancing could suggest alterations to pressured families.

Balancing helps illuminate another dilemma regarding children. Historically, children's contribution to the American family has run the gamut from complete exploitation of the young to optimum benefit for all. A twentieth-century trend has kept children in school longer and delayed their entry into the workplace. As a result, they must share household chores in order to learn responsibility early. Recently, however, increased employment of adult family members through choice and need has thrust countless youngsters into situations where they carry a heavier domestic load than is appropriate for them. So many babysitting and cooking duties can be shifted onto youthful shoulders that the child becomes an unpaid housekeeper. Latchkey kids like Tanya are sometimes communicating to counselors and school officials their wish to do what they are capable of handling and no more.

As a decision maker proceeds through Step 2, she will hope to increase her alternatives and enlarge her opportunities. She may decide to seek the advice of an expert if time permits and circumstances dictate. She may make use of the resources of books and community programs to add to her information and understanding. At this stage she will also listen for signals that come from her vital center. These promptings could lead her to develop better alternatives. Additionally, with an active mind and an expectant heart, a person facing choices turns to God. She could receive help as well from persons close to her. If a decision maker is attentive to these varied sources of support and guidance, she may find herself drawn to consider a new direction she had not seen earlier.

Going a Step Further:

1. Obtain expert advice or information about a personal matter that you need to handle well. What was the easiest part of the process? the most frustrating?
2. Assemble all of the information that your family would need if you should die today. Check to make certain that your will is up-to-date and clearly reflects your wishes.
3. Read G. Victor Hallman and Jerry S. Rosenbloom, *Personal Financial Planning* (New York: McGraw-Hill Book Co., 1983), then take

a comprehensive look at how you allocate the financial resources you have.

4. Read John C. Crystal and Richard N. Bolles, *Where Do I Go From Here With My Life?* (Berkeley: Ten Speed Press, 1980) or Eleanor Berman, *Re-Entering: Successful Back-to-Work Strategies for Women Seeking a Fresh Start* (New York: Crown Publishers, 1980) and assess your vocational status.

7

Step 3 in Decision Making:
ENVISION THE OUTCOME

As she completes her list of alternatives, a woman approaches the third step of the process. She must visualize the results of her decision making. Envisioning the outcome is essential for two reasons: to strengthen one's sense of both possibilities and obstacles. If the individual has followed the first two steps clearly and completely, she will already have expended some mental effort. She will have reviewed where she stands at this juncture in her life. She may have new regard for her strengths and aptitudes and have considered the environment that will enhance these. Moreover she will have told those close to her about her desire to change and reckoned with their reactions.

If a woman now envisages what she could become, this mental picture will increase her chance of succeeding with the change. Sometimes all a decision maker has at the outset is this vision. While no one can take it away from her, she is the only one who can make it real. Also, the sooner she can see inwardly what she wants to do, the sooner she can begin to act. At Step 3 a decision maker realizes that, in a real sense, her future is in her hands. Some find this assumption inspiring while others view it as a burden. If a woman can achieve and maintain a mental picture of how things could be, that vision could carry her into the fourth step, taking effective action.

Visions are mistakenly thought to be the sole province of mystics, and creativity is narrowly associated with artists. Why is creative vision so important to a decision maker? If the change or decision is substantial at all, it will require time and effort. As will be seen, it could bring on confusion and induce anxiety. Someone with a clear vision of the intended outcome can better handle both. Whether we are wholly aware of it or not, any normal person is endowed with the capacity to visualize the future. No one functions effectively if she loses the power to look ahead and to move beyond the present moment. It is especially important for a decision maker to cultivate her capacity for vision. If her decision is one of the so-called life choices, it will require complex, repeated envisioning in order to turn out well.

Having a clear mental picture of the outcome can preserve it through difficulties. Obstacles and setbacks inevitably will arise. A decision maker will reappraise matters on occasion. Throughout the process of change she keeps that vision of the intended result before her. It is at Step 3 that she tries to become aware of the forces that could sabotage her objective. Anyone attempting a change wishes to be cognizant of these—even if, on occasion, they appear as rather harsh realities. On the other hand, when obstacles and uncertainties cloud a decision maker's view entirely, she will lose sight of the tremendous possibilities for a future that is—as yet—undetermined.

As we follow the thoughts of two women with decisions to make, it is obvious that visualizing can markedly affect the outcome. The first, trying to decide whether to become a mother, considers a choice that will affect her for the rest of her life. Once the child is born, her own identity is permanently altered. Her daily functioning will be modified for many years to come. She wants to foresee both physical and psychological transformations. She begins by thinking about pregnancy. It can be a time of well-being for a healthy woman. Nonetheless, she gives thought to possible problems and learns in advance exactly how her body will change both before and after the birth of the baby. Rather than relying on hearsay, she and her husband decide to read on their own. They agree that, if she becomes pregnant, they will attend some class rather than depend on recollections of friends or comments of a busy obstetrician or midwife.

Next the young woman envisions what life could be like after delivery. Assuming all goes well, the two of them will be introducing a completely unknowable element into the equation of everydayness when they bring the baby home. Even a fit, healthy new mother experiences drastic demands on her stamina. She imagines rearranging her routine to account for this fact. She sees that it would be wise to adopt a flexible attitude for some months. When women fail to account for the enormous energy drain of motherhood, they begin to despair of ever again resuming the life they once enjoyed. The feeling can stem from simple, prolonged tiredness. She and her husband conclude that only a clear view of what to expect will enable them to keep perspective and a sense of humor—even if the baby swaps day and night for months!

Envisioning the outcome of a pregnancy is complicated when the woman is a working wife. Polls report that contemporary women overwhelmingly declare an intention to have children *and* retain their jobs. When women approach the possibility of combining work and motherhood, they would be well advised to think long and hard about the outcome. Signs are appearing that employers are accommodating to female workers who choose to take a maternity leave, then return to the job. Such employees no longer will lose pension rights when they are away for childbirth and/or child rearing. Firms may now provide child-care assistance to employees as a nontaxable benefit. Some working mothers take advantage of flexible working hours to fulfill parental responsibilities as they keep up at the office.

However, it would be foolish to ignore the problems which this decision can create, particularly if the prospective mother holds a demanding job. Women in a career track say especially they weigh the question of timing carefully. While they report that they do not wish to go childless too long, they want to feel that they are interrupting employment at a propitious time. Some recalled learning about a pending promotion or promise of enlarged responsibilities only after telling their superiors that they were requesting maternity leave. Even more common is difficult readjustment following the leave. A few weeks of being with a baby full-time can create amazing bonds. Once back on the job, the mother can feel torn by these attachments. She may reconcile this conflict in time but at first miss her baby so much that her work performance is affected.

Working mothers inevitably wrestle with the thorny question of child care. It is a factor that is hard to envision when deciding whether to have a baby or not. Reliable child care of a quality that will satisfy new parents is expensive and hard to obtain. Such facilities cannot expand fast enough to meet demand. Presently several million preschoolers attend some kind of day care or formal programs that free working parents from the homefront.

The prospective mother and father will want to be mindful of another dilemma. Fathers who wish to share parenting equally find it discouraging to encounter prejudices against this intention. Expectations remain strong that men will put their jobs before their children. Unless each parent is fortunate enough to have a flexible work routine, they must turn to day care. Single working mothers do not have the opportunity of even considering shared parenthood.

In spite of all these difficulties, the task of Step 3 is to catch a vision of fresh possibilities as well as to be advised of obstacles. In addition to a wife becoming a mother, this couple can be transformed into a family. That development can be a singular source of joy. When thinking about the prospect, however, the couple should realize that the process takes much more time than they might suspect. The creation of a real family is very time consuming. Two busy, preoccupied individuals intent on enlarging their respective paychecks will want to review their priorities. They may decide that the promise of building a stable, joyous family life is worth more than driving endlessly toward career advancement. Having an opportunity to answer a child's questions, watch his or her growing pains, and together manage the big snafus and surprising small pleasures are marvelous outgrowths of this decision.

Two people who decide to create a family also raise the possibility of reflecting some of the attributes of transcendent love. A couple weighing parenthood might want to reflect on the idea that the "initial sense of the presence of God is ordinarily mediated and subsequently reinforced by familial experiences."[1] With some imagination, a man and woman can set to work building a family structure that allows for forgiveness, reconciliation, and acceptance among its members. Just as healing or reconciliation are slow processes, so is the creation of a strong family. While it may seem like a rarity today, such a family is possible through mutual commitment. On occasion a family can even point toward the ultimate triumph of God's creative love over destructive forces in the cosmos.

When a couple starts to change into a family, the process alters their view of time. They expect to remain a unit for an entire generation. Statistics warn that this is, at best, a precarious probability, so they consider ways to avoid coming apart under future pressure. They may look at their relationship in a new light. Is it strong enough to accommodate the transformation? Can they make some adjustments that will better enable this family they are creating to withstand shocks, struggles, even success down the road? Shifting personal relationships from a contingency basis to one that is permanent is never easy today. The two persons involved simply have to spend time envisioning what might happen—not only during the first months of parenthood—but for the next twenty years.

The decision to become a family opens the way to eventualities that are as awesome as they are fulfilling. Conservative estimates indicate that raising a child to age eighteen costs more than $200,000. Parental concerns evolve from arranging child care to doctoring chicken pox to helping with homework. Eventually they will see their offspring drawn into the adolescent subculture. They will watch a child embrace the world of rock music and become a teenage driver.

Through it all they can take pleasure in being together and gain growing understanding of the power of love. St. Paul was right. Love never fails. It can survive overscheduling, pressures, indifference, even alienation to renew itself in ways that on occasion leave a family amazed. When a couple envisions becoming a family, they should be mindful of the transforming power of love.

In a second situation, a woman suddenly left alone in her fifties must envision a different kind of future. A vision of change has been forced upon her by events, and she must struggle to bring it into focus. For quite a while she may doubt that she can do this. Eventually she must reckon with what has happened and start to envision the remainder of her life. In a very real sense she will become the elderly woman she visualizes. She will go through a long succession of choices and changes in the months and years ahead. With positive mental pictures of the last third of her life, she could plan a future that will be rich and unique though different from what she anticipated.

An older woman in this situation may find it necessary to act before she has gained any clear vision of the future at all. Some unavoidable steps will have to be taken immediately. If such a decision maker is at least aware of the need to envision her future, then perhaps she can avoid proceeding far on an unintended course. Just knowing that she needs creative plans in order to make the most of the remainder of life could help her to go slowly. After she has worked through the process of grieving or separation somewhat, she will be more ready to contemplate what lies ahead. At the outset, however, she may find some ideas helpful. One is that in the face of an unexpected solitary existence, a woman can learn to be alone without being lonely.

Living alone without loneliness calls for certain inner attitudes and some special qualities of the spirit. One of these is the ability to remain open to life. While she is still grieving, a woman may not see how she can manage this. As she moves ahead, however, she can aim for a balance between exploring new options and sustaining reliable patterns of thinking and doing. She might also wish to renew some activity that gave satisfaction in the past. Women who attempt something that represents a complete change in their later years can attain notable results. Lillian Carter, mother of the former president, was an elderly widow when she decided to join the Peace Corps. Those to whom a new vocation seems farfetched can concentrate on a special talent. Author Helen Santmyer was eighty-eight years old when she received national recognition and Book-of-the-Month-Club selection for a novel that she began in the 1920s.

The difference between being alone and being lonely often seems to lie in the degree of one's involvement with others. A woman may live alone and look after herself, but she is not necessarily by herself. Loneliness arises when, on the other hand, a person is isolated and often alienated from other people. When an individual's outside contacts shrivel up and die, alienation breeds. Thus, when envisioning her future, the solitary older woman will want to attend carefully to her personal relationships. She may start to strengthen those that offer conviviality and support. Women in this situation report that well-meaning family and friends fail to grasp their need for enlarged social ties. Instead they find themselves excluded from the plans of "couple" friends and are forced to seek single companions.

Sometimes older women who have been primarily homebound for decades decide to enlarge their tenuous ties to the community and wider world. They make new commitments to causes that lie outside private concerns or share in the work of a group that interests them. Older adults who decide to become increasingly active in the social sphere fill a desperate need. The ranks of community volunteers have been thinned by women's shift into gainful employment. All such organizations would like to see more willing helpers with time to spare. Besides traditional volunteer outlets, some interesting new opportunities are evolving for older women. One is the program of surrogate grandparents. The relationship of grandparents to young people has been prized by families for generations. Now it has acquired new dimensions. The lives of old and young are enriched when communities start the popular program.

An older woman who wishes to avoid loneliness may find outlets that are closed to younger women in her circumstances and, in fact, were not available to her earlier in life. Countless younger women who are widowed or divorced have no choice but to become the primary breadwinner and take a full-time job. Someone in her fifties may decide that she has sufficient resources to supplement these with a part-time position or, better yet, a shared job. Also she can take advantage of the growing opportunities for education in the form of self-enrichment. Travel also breaks down walls between a solitary woman and the world. These two options combine beautifully in programs such as Elderhostel which gives an interim of change with intellectual stimulation.

Any vision which an older woman shapes requires an underlying foundation of good health and financial security. Physical well-being can be a great positive influence in the life and plans of someone past fifty. Women who understand and practice fitness will sustain higher energy levels for travel and new activities. The health of elderly persons can be profoundly affected by proper nutrition. A good diet can have a bearing on whether or not they develop certain afflictions ranging from cancer to osteoporosis. Even if a woman learns that she has osteoporosis or certain gynecological problems, for example, these ailments need not become chronic troubles. Good care and early treatment can overcome the effects of many complaints associated with aging females.

Even so, a woman envisions both the benefits and the potentially harmful side effects of a course of treatment. For example, if the woman suddenly on her own is also experiencing menopause, she may seek medical help for its symptoms. One of the proposed alternatives will likely be estrogen therapy. She has already established that preserving a good state of health overall is a high priority with her. She has envisioned a vigorous old age. This vision plus background information about estrogen therapy may influence her to rule out the option. She could decide that it carries unacceptable risks and will only postpone physiological adjustments that are presently causing her uncomfortable symptoms.

Just as she cultivates health habits that foster wellness and energy, she must acquire financial resources to remain self-sufficient. As already indicated, solitary older women are in a population category that is increasingly vulnerable to poverty and economic dependency. Any person in this category must visualize what constitutes economic well-being for her and try to maintain that level. All the time she must bear in mind that it might be very hard to regain any lost ground financially. Envisioning the financial needs of old age can prove to be a demanding task for a solitary woman in her early fifties. Even so, she would be starting this effort late according to most financial authorities. Experts caution Americans to initiate retirement planning while they are in their thirties. Even if the envisioned change involves nothing more than a different residence, that step must be planned carefully. Many desirable retirement complexes have waiting periods that stretch out for years. The cost of a new location could be prohibitive without advance preparation. Looking ahead means that a woman will plan ahead for a satisfying old age.

An older person who has habitually shared all of her time with others may have difficulty adjusting to planning future time for herself. Although her time is her own in ways she never experienced heretofore, she may not desire this freedom of choice. She could refuse to manage her time purposefully. Perhaps unconsciously resentful over her loss, she can simply "mark time" until months, even years, have passed. On the other hand, she may be able to view her singleness as an opportunity rather than a terrible condition. She then could try to make her remaining time into a period of growth. She can refuse to let a precious gift of time slip through her fingers.

If an older person can make this mental breakthrough about future time, she will start to visualize some plans. After all, she could be determining what will happen to her during a period of time as long as that from her birth to adulthood! The mental pictures she holds of her life in one year, five years, twenty-five years may well come true. She tries to balance the gains and losses of her life. Holidays or special anniversaries could bring moments of unaccountable fury that things will never be as they once were. At such times she will try to strengthen her sense of uniqueness and hold that against her sorrow. As the periodic shocks occur at longer and longer intervals, she may discover that she is becoming the elderly person she visualized. Even though alone, she is vigorous and productive. Accepting the imperative of choosing, she plans and moves ahead.

Regardless of age or circumstance, a woman will begin to feel the need for perseverance at Step 3 of decision making. The fresh start could be complicated. The desired change may be a major one. If so, obstacles to fulfillment of these plans will be sizeable. In the last half of the process of deciding a woman must deal successfully with barriers and pitfalls or lose the goal she now has in mind. A decision maker gains a stronger grip on perseverance by being certain she truly needs the change or fresh start and that it will occur in manageable phases. That assurance will get her started and keep her persisting. Perseverance grows when a woman has promised herself to aim for greater satisfaction and well-being generally.

Rhea is an example of a woman who could not easily envision the outcome of a decision which she needed to make but with help did find the perseverance to move through Step 3. At thirty-four she had been married, divorced, and was now engaged again. Then Rhea abruptly concluded that matrimony would be a mistake. She told herself that she was only trying to bolster her identity through depending on another man. For the first time in her life, Rhea really wanted to rid herself of the conviction that she was helpless. She knew that on its present basis, the relationship with her fiancé would not have led to a strong, happy marriage. Therefore Rhea felt no regret about breaking off with her boyfriend.

She was still in limbo psychologically, however. She had the nagging impression that she had not really launched her drive for autonomy. One evening her roommate told Rhea they should abandon their apartment and find separate housing. "You know you depended on Mike all those years. You stopped yourself before you hooked up with Terry and used him as a crutch. I'm not going to let you hang onto me indefinitely. You were dead right when you decided it was time to try your wings. Now put your money where your mouth is."

Their talk convinced Rhea that she must visualize a tangible step flowing from her inner decision to "try her wings." She decided that, as proof of her commitment to independence, she would get a place of her own for the first time. Other friends backed up her roommate. They tried to encourage Rhea by insisting that she had been selling herself short. A cousin who was a realtor talked with her about her future plans. He persuaded Rhea that she should consider buying a condominium rather than paying further rent. The effort to locate and arrange financing for a unit that she could afford did not come easily for Rhea. Once she had finally moved, however, Rhea could look back and see the importance of visualizing the intended outcome of her change. Establishing a residence of her own somehow broke the long pattern of dependency.

Time and struggle were required in Rhea's fresh start. Admitting the need to find a separate self was only a preliminary step. Rhea had always believed that living alone would be a last resort for her when all of her "others" failed her. Having assumed for years that she would be miserable in solitary quarters, Rhea knew that, if she could bring a vision of herself as a homeowner to actuality, it would be a significant breakthrough for her. Her relative in the real estate business gave Rhea a little added incentive when he pointed out that purchasing a residence offered substantial financial benefits as well as the psychological fulfillment she sought. Rhea had many uneasy moments as she attended to details of purchasing the condominium, furnishing it, and arranging her move.

After some months this woman could say honestly that she felt better than she had in years. She even began to think of being single in a positive way. Marriage would be fine if she found a man with whom she really wanted to share her new life. At the same time, Rhea knew that she could enjoy the arrangement she had made on her own. She began to view singleness as some of her contemporaries did. Rhea had looked upon it as a negative, even tragic, condition. Now she saw it as a time when, unencumbered with domestic responsibilities, she could explore who she is and what the world is like.

Fortunately, stereotypes of single women have faded recently. Once people gave very negative labels to women who chose not to marry. They were warped spinsters or frustrated old maids, often treated as unwelcome dependents. Now single women attain both economic and psychological independence. For the first time in her life, Rhea had a vision of both.

Like many other successful decision makers, this woman planned a change which she could reasonably handle. Rhea did not get carried away with either her possibilities or her obstacles. Following the suggestions of many clinical psychologists and counselors, she kept her life simple at the time and made her transition in small steps. If Rhea had moved to another city, changed jobs, and tried to acquire a new circle of friends all at once, her attempt at independence might have failed. By limiting her fresh start to the residential aspect of life only, Rhea enhanced the chance of success. Moreover, she chose that part of her life over which she had greatest control. She left untouched for the moment those areas where others played a large part in determining things. The ultimate responsibility did rest with her in this case, and her strategy gave her self-confidence a maximum boost.

Perhaps one reason why individuals are cautioned about attempting too much change simultaneously is that decision making often arises as a result of some crisis. Doctors have made long-term studies of the stress produced by various crises or life changes. As a result of voluminous case histories, they developed a social readjustment rating scale, assigning weight to events such as retirement, pregnancy, divorce. Individuals who accumulated a high score on the scale in a short time and responded badly to the changes often fell victim to illness or disease. Such research projects have helped to illuminate possible links between stressful change, personal attitudes, and immunology.

The information from these studies may caution decision makers not to allow stress they may already be enduring to reach intolerable levels. On the whole this book seeks to encourage women to use actively more of their abilities and emphasizes possibilities. Yet a word of warning is in order. During a major transition a decision maker may want to keep the number of new variables to a minimum. She can then concentrate her energy on taking reasonable steps, and she must remain sensitive to the stress that change brings.

In addition, Step 3 of the decision-making process is the time to anticipate opposition to the change or choice. A woman can face opposition from those around her, from broader social pressures, or even both—as Debbie's decision reveals. Debbie was an energetic twenty-year-old. When she told her parents of her intention to become an electrician, they begged her to forget the idea. Her mother said that construction sites were no place for a woman. Her father warned her about traditional union opposition to women in such trades. Even in locales with open shops, she might not be hired and could expect a hard time on the job. Because she tried for a vocation not often associated with women, Debbie fought sexual

stereotyping at every turn. Her friends teased her. Working conditions would never be easy. It was shocking to realize what she was
up against. Only 2 percent of the country's electricians are women.

She decided to focus on simply not giving up. She could see that
she was about the only one in her life who found her plan feasible.
The obstacles were obvious, but she was not yet sure what would
constitute success for her. All she could do at this point was refuse
to quit. Eventually Debbie decided that many success stories could
be told mainly in terms of refusal to abandon a goal. Opposition to
her vocational plan was hard on her, and she had never thought of
herself as a combative person. Still, most alternatives did not appeal, so she resolved that she was going to have the last word on
her job future. No outsider was going to label her efforts as a
failure.

Debbie's story illustrates one way to face obstacles to a decision.
At the outset she found tough going. Yet she had a clear sense of
the kind of person she was and what work she wanted to pursue.
Her friends would have described Debbie as a live wire (no pun intended). This temperament helped, as did the stick-to-it attitude
which she adopted. She accepted as givens that she wanted to work
in an unconventional job and that her emotional mother and pro-
tective father would try to change her mind. Down the road, she
might adjust her sights. For the time being, she stuck to her idea
despite the difficulty.

Often female decision makers must show just such a degree of
perseverance if they are to succeed, because traditional socialization
of women can obstruct the process of deciding. Below the conscious
level of planning and taking action are powerful forces that hold
back many females. Long-term trends are clearly directing women
toward more active choosing and capitalizing on opportunities, yet
the weight of traditional rearing and roles slows their steps. This
socialization manifests itself in several ways during the decision-
making process. For instance, a woman can be excessively concerned with being "nice" even when other behavior would be more
appropriate and helpful. As a result of her upbringing, she considers it "unfeminine" to express her anger directly and goes to great
lengths to avoid a conflict.

This particular "feminine" attitude can rob a decision maker of the courage of her convictions, as Dot's case demonstrates. For months Dot stood by while her husband and daughter contended over the young woman's idea that she should stop working in her father's insurance agency and move to another state. Dot habitually served as mediator between these two hotheads. From childhood she had exhibited a soothing personality. Now she was reluctant to abandon a role she prized and take sides. Her best judgment told her, however, it was a mistake to let the struggle continue. If Dot told her daughter and husband exactly what she thought, both would become angry with her. It was very hard for her to assert herself, but finally Dot's common sense triumphed over her perennial "niceness." She saw that the entire family would benefit if she would be blunt and intervene decisively for once. Once tempers cooled, her husband and daughter agreed.

In a further example, Carolyn's story reveals how a woman's desire to be "nice" deters her from giving consideration to her own needs. Accustomed always to doing for her significant others, Carolyn felt guilty for even thinking of doing something only for herself. She had married young and borne three children in quick succession. Her husband had no objections when she raised the possibility of becoming a coed at thirty-five. Their children were another matter: sometimes they pouted, other times they stormed, one even let her grades slide. In every way possible they put their mother on the defensive.

Carolyn definitely needed to do something on her own. She had never seemed so alive and competent before. Yet her guilty reaction to the children very nearly cost Carolyn her chance for a diploma. In her second semester she joined a study group and stayed on campus late once a week to work with them. Another mother in the group alerted Carolyn to what was happening. All of her children's lives Carolyn had considered only their needs. Now they were adroitly creating guilty feelings in their mother, and these reactions jeopardized her dream. Carolyn fought hard to counter the feeling that she had abandoned them, especially when her exams took precedence over the family's annual spring camping trip.

Later in the course of breaking out of a twenty-year homebound role Carolyn exhibited another behavioral tendency of traditional women: self-doubt. By now she had gotten her college diploma and was scouting for jobs. When she received an unexpected offer, Carolyn was momentarily swamped. The self-confidence which she had developed by returning to school and simultaneously running a household seemed to vanish. She felt a pervasive distrust of her ability to plan and take action.

This lapse into self-doubt disturbed Carolyn. She thought she had put many of her old attitudes behind her. The company obviously wanted her to take the job, and she had every indication that she could learn the ropes and do quite well. She had laid the groundwork of a new routine with her husband and teenagers as a middle-aged college student. Yet at the same time she drew back from accepting the prize that hard work had brought her. She questioned her ability to manage new demands and found the prospect unnerving. Carefully, she set about working through her negative feelings.

Carolyn's response emphasizes the importance of taking preventive action to preserve a goal. Anticipating factors that could sabotage a successful outcome and acting to offset these is essential. Honesty and realism are central to good decisions. They keep a woman from overestimating or underestimating her chance of success. After all, false optimism can imperil plans as well as active opposition can. The process of decision making points up the value of taking a broad view. Awareness of the past gives a woman strength and the impetus to move ahead. The notion of creative vision helps her to shape her future actively. As will be seen at the conclusion of this study, vision and purposeful action can combine effectively in the public as well as the private realm of life.

Going a Step Further:

1. Give further consideration to the decision you identified in chapter 4. Write about obstacles to success with the goal and note positive evidence that you will succeed.

2. What is the most frustrating aspect of parenting today? How is parenting easier than it was two generations ago?

3. Read Carol Gilligan, *In a Different Voice: Psychological Theory and Women's Development* (Cambridge: Harvard University Press, 1982) or Judith Bardwick, *In Transition: How Feminism, Sexual Liberation, and the Search for Self-Fulfillment Have Altered Our Lives* (New York: Holt, Rinehart, & Winston, 1979) for insights into the psychology of women.

4. Read Jane Porcino, *Growing Older, Getting Better: A Handbook for Women in the Second Half of Life* (Reading: Addison-Wesley Publishing Co., 1983) or Nancy C. Baker, *New Lives for Former Wives: Displaced Homemakers* (New York: Anchor, 1980) and think about making a fresh start yourself.

8

Step 4 in Decision Making:
TAKE ACTION

"It's time to act." How do many women react when they hear that order? Whether it comes from a spouse, employer, doctor, or an inner voice, often decision makers feel they are not ready to act. Timing presents them with a special dilemma. They ask themselves whether they should choose now or try to identify other alternatives. Could they wait for a more propitious moment or better circumstances? Would it be wise to consider the decision just a little longer? None of the three steps in the decision-making process analyzed previously will amount to anything unless action is taken. If no decision results and no moves occur, then all of the preliminary effort will have been wasted.

People can prepare for a decision or undertake a fresh start, then deceive themselves about this fourth step. Perhaps they run the decision around in their heads for so long that they lose sight of the fact that action is NOT more mental activity. Worrying about a decision often prompts an individual to discuss it with friends or relatives. Talking over decisions with friends can be positive and helpful but is no substitute for proper action. Maybe women hesitate at the fourth step of decision making because of age-old female behavior patterns. The "man of action," fabled in literature and history, has, after all, no mirror image among the opposite sex.

All too often, however, women are forced to act, and as the following example makes clear, must be certain they are taking the most appropriate steps. Molly lost her husband in an automobile accident. One of the resolves that this woman in her late thirties carried from the tragedy was a determination to obtain adequate insurance. Her husband, she discovered, was underinsured in almost every area where people use insurance to handle exposure to risk. In order to protect her future and that of her children, Molly investigated, in turn, each category of insurance. When she had decided on the level of coverage, she ordered policies that were adequate and up-to-date. Molly could only wish that she and her husband had made this review and taken action before his fatal accident.

Life insurance, Molly learned, is a field in transition. Once it came in two basic forms—term and permanent. Term insurance provides basic protection to those who depend on a person's income. It has no residual value and thus carries smaller premiums than other forms of life insurance. Therefore term insurance is often chosen by younger couples with lower income but the need to protect a family against loss of that income. This could be the only way a family avoids catastrophe when a breadwinner dies. Permanent (or whole) life insurance once was regarded as security for one's dependents as well as a form of investment. Recent inflation and introduction of many new fixed income investment instruments changed the latter notion. Many insurance companies have responded by altering policies and introducing new products to attract customers on the grounds that permanent life insurance is more than a form of savings.

Molly had never thought that life insurance was necessary for her, but now she saw the need for protecting the family should she also die or become disabled. If Molly were able to return to work full-time, group life insurance policies obtained through an employer would yield many advantages. These advantages parallel those of group health policies. Moreover, it is best to buy life insurance while young. After about age forty-five policies may not even be obtainable or only through prohibitively high cost. Equally important to Molly as a prospective employee was income continuation insurance. Estimates are that one-third of all Americans now in their thirties will be disabled for a long period during their careers. Half of these disabilities will last up to two years. Income continuation insurance is a sometimes overlooked but necessary form of protection against tragedy.

A woman like Molly must also carry insurance on real and personal property. However modest or grand it is, property should be insured at a level that would enable an individual to replace what could be lost or destroyed. Experts warn Americans that homeowner's insurance should total 80 percent of current replacement costs. Otherwise, money from the insurance company will not allow one to replace the loss. Coverage should be comprehensive or "all-risk." People often fail to insure important new purchases (such as a personal computer) or increase coverage when the worth of valuables accrues. Automobile and personal liability policies frequently fall in the underinsured category as well. Molly could not afford all of the coverage she would have liked to purchase but knew that she must protect her family against the greatest risks, then cover potential smaller losses insofar as possible.

Despite determination to take appropriate action, anxiety can pervade the life of anyone facing a decision. This is especially true if the choice is being made under pressure or all the alternatives seem to involve risk. A woman can become gripped by some manifestation of anxiety almost before she realizes what is happening. In this state individuals find themselves hoping for an out—even a miracle—that will allow them to avoid acting. Some admit that they balk until absolutely forced into taking some step. Others tell themselves they must wait until a more favorable time. They want just the right moment to make a fresh start or try a change. Decision makers must somehow meet anxiety head-on. Anyone who understands anxiety stands a better chance of countering whatever effect it is having on her life.

For example, anxiety can produce a multitude of alibis that

swim into the mind and deflect the best of intentions. Alibis assail any woman about to act. After the morning's first cup of coffee she thinks of reasons why her plan cannot possibly work. She is tempted by the "Cinderella syndrome." Like Cinderella, she sighs, I too am enveloped in the mess of everyday. Yet no fairy godmother is ever likely to find her way to this suburban split level. In this state of mind asking God for help seems foolish to her. Surely God has a full schedule this morning, she concludes, when the whole world seems heaving toward doom. She asks herself if God is likely to provide a quick boost to the plans of a tentative, depressed, American female?

Dread of pain, another manifestation of anxiety, may also be the pretext for stopping short of action. A woman wonders why she should get her hopes up if, in the end, she will be rejected and feel worse than ever? This type of rationalization can beset a woman of any age but is very hard to counter past one's fortieth birthday. A new employee is pessimistic, for instance, about gaining acceptance into an office where most of the other female workers look like girls to her. Another woman shies away from taking college courses if the other coeds are her daughter's friends. Still another cancels plans to join a health club after one look in the full-length mirror. The forces of gravity have already done too much damage, she decides. The prospect of working out in a body suit is too distressing to accept.

When the pending decision follows a time of personal crisis, avoidance of further pain is a powerful influence on individuals. Well-meaning friends may even offer the excuse before the decision maker expresses it herself. "Considering what you've been through, why would you want to put more pressure on yourself?" they ask. Their argument does sound plausible to her. After the devastation, she has hardly gotten back to her normal level of functioning. It would be too much to attempt something new. "I probably did well not to fall apart completely last year," she tells herself. "Best leave the adventures to the lucky women who haven't received the shock I got. If I ran into trouble, I'd probably have to go on Valium again."

Sometimes the decision-making process fizzles out because

anxiety produces unpleasant physical symptoms. Knowing that such butterflies or palpitations are likely to occur can help a woman take them in stride rather than give up after a few flutters. A transition period or deciding time sets off panic in some individuals and depression in others. The physical symptoms of this anxiety are hard to handle in either case because they can be very debilitating. While it is not possible to discuss anxiety's physiological manifestations in much detail, any decision maker should be alert to its effects.

For instance, during times of unresolved dilemmas a person can become possessed with great nervous energy. In this guise anxiety drives a woman to frenetic activity and scatters her life force. By day she is unable to concentrate effort on the action needed to reach her goal. At night her mind continues to race. The sleep which could help this restlessness eludes her. A vicious cycle of exhaustion and hyperactivity sets in. This form of anxiety produces other behavioral changes besides consuming jumpiness. A person's appetite may dwindle, or she could indulge in overeating or excessive drinking. She can experience pain from tense muscles and joints, even develop cardiovascular problems.

Sometimes anxiety has a depressing effect. Misery pulls a woman down and makes decision making impossible. She begins to withdraw from activity into isolation. Rather than taking action to change or enlarge her life, she does less than usual. She loses interest in the progress already made. Depression rooted in anxiety bears bitter fruit like feelings of worthlessness and alienation. Without help, a woman suffering in this manner may become vulnerable to despair. Christian tradition stretching back to the early church rightly identified despair as a critical condition that carries people away from others and from God. As we have seen, good decisions and sound choices are rooted in honesty and realism. Anxiety robs a person of these two attitudes. It chokes off one's sense of possibilities. Anxiety also can blind one to the goodness of life.

How does a woman blunt the force of anxiety? She stands a better chance if she remains aware of the problem's potential for harm. After all, if anxiety thwarts a necessary decision, the individual could ultimately be worse off than ever. She will also want to keep in mind the benefits of good health habits—both physical and mental. Careful attention to these can help reverse the ill effects of anxiety. The basics are balanced meals, ample rest, and extra exercise. Anyone will discover that increased physical fitness measurably improves her ability to keep working on a change or a new goal.

A period of uncertainty and exploration when an individual is anxiously scanning the horizon is a good time to employ stress management. Such techniques directly ameliorate the nervous symptoms that decision making and change often cause. A variety of relaxation techniques target specific problems. Some will reduce muscle tension. Others will alleviate breathing difficulties. Stress management exercises may counteract sudden blood pressure elevations that plague people under stress. Decision making can also interrupt sleep patterns or cause gastric upsets. Stress management helps a person under pressure retain the benefits of rest and nutrition. Both are essential if one is to weigh problems realistically and make sound choices.

A daily time of quiet solitude also reduces the risk that anxiety poses to the spirit of someone trying to decide. Moments of reflection and renewal are more important than ever when an individual feels harassed and confused. Reflecting silently, she gains a stronger sense of self. She may find that simplifying her life during the decision-making period helps. Trying to handle too much at once will only raise the level of anxiety. If her normal schedule is crammed, she could eliminate some activities and concentrate on the more satisfying outlets. If her usual pace is hectic, she will slow down and relax often.

Yet a decision maker must guard against the temptation to stop altogether. At no point should she long lose sight of action, even in the throes of anxiety. For instance, if she is subject to nervous manifestations, she could channel some of this extra energy. She can plan, investigate alternatives, or do some troubleshooting about her decision. Harnessing one's restlessness helps maintain self-control. It lowers the panic level. On the other hand, if a woman falls prey to the depressive side of anxiety, she may doubt her ability to act at all. What can she do to gain momentum even to seek professional help?

She can start by reminding herself that she *can* act. This sense of one's own initiative is sometimes all that a person has going for her. It can be enough, however, to prevent her from giving up without a try. She may eventually have to go to outside helpers, but ultimately she will bear responsibility for the change anyway. Grasping the crucial importance of personal volition can be a real breakthrough to a decision maker. Perhaps most importantly, it helps a person see that others will not control the outcome of the situation. They can neither secure her personal future nor prevent her from changing her prospects. Fresh understanding of responsibility also changes the way an individual looks at both obstacles and opportunities.

Perhaps the recollection of an alcoholic will illustrate how action can go forward under very unfavorable circumstances. The woman recalled realizing that within her was the power to start to throw off this dependency. Her thoughts, she said, ran something like this: "Alcohol is the cause of my troubles, my suffering. My drinking is ruining my life. I stand to lose family, friends, job, whatever sense of self I have unless I seek treatment. It is possible that I could get help and reverse this terrible downward spiral. I will have to choose to do this, however." She learned that not only would she have to take action initially, but she would also have to maintain responsibility throughout the long recovery process.

Thanks to scientific research, an alcoholic need no longer feel that she has to fight her disease with will power alone. Treatment centers offer multifaceted programs of help and information. Nonetheless, an alcoholic must choose to begin treatment. It is often harder for a woman to start the long, uneven road to recovery. If she drinks mainly at home alone, her family may avoid facing up to her growing dependency. For a long time she may delude herself about how much and why she drinks. If personal pressures or disruptions are great, she could continue to blame others for her excessive drinking. One in ten Americans develops a severe drinking problem. Alcoholism is sometimes called this country's number one health concern. Since 1966, when the American Medical Association recognized alcoholism as a disease, health professionals' understanding of the problem has grown enormously. Yet even though her physician, relatives, friends, and her boss may plead with an alcoholic to seek treatment, she is the only person who can take that action.

In another situation we can see that at the outset a decision maker's determination to regain control need only be great enough to start her moving. She does not have to be sure that she will sweep to complete success. Learning the secret of will power helped Angie, a twenty-seven-year-old woman, resolve a painful problem at work. Looking back, Angie admitted that self-initiative was the key to dealing with the sexual harassment from her boss. When she got the job, it meant that she and her husband could begin shopping for a home. She readily learned the office routine and liked the work. Then her troubles began. "At first I thought I was imagining things," Angie recalled. "Mr. Davis struck me as being so prim and proper. As far as you could get from my childhood image of a dirty old man." Yet the supervisor's attentions persisted.

The remainder of Angie's story shows how easily outcomes can turn on a person's will to do something. She tried a polite scolding. Mr. Davis grew increasingly specific about what could happen if she resisted his advances. Angie and her husband were already working with a realtor who was showing the couple condominiums and checking into financing for them. Angie grew sick inside. There seemed to be no way she could avoid misfortune. One afternoon an older employer found her crying in a back room and asked some sympathetic questions. From their conversation Angie learned that before she was hired Mr. Davis had approached a young employee in another department. With Angie's placement directly under his jurisdiction, she became the sole object of the man's harassment. Angie called on the employee after work and asked about her trouble with Davis. She had no assurance that talking to the other victim would lead to a solution, but Angie was determined to do something.

When she took that initiative, Angie could not have foreseen a successful resolution of this problem. On her own she triggered a chain of events that led to intervention by the company's personnel manager. Eventually the action enabled her to remain on the job. Sexism in the workplace, she learned, is inescapable. It varies from the blatant harassment that Angie faced to more subtle forms such as a boss asking a female employee to run personal errands for him. Women must learn all of their legal rights as workers. They have to stay abreast of wage and hour laws and know what is the minimum wage for various jobs. In case of unemployment, they should avail themselves of the services of the local Employment Security Commission. Finally, women must be willing to unite in efforts to make the workplace safer and fairer for all females.

Angie's behavior also reveals something about confidence at Step 4. Confidence sometimes is mistaken for an inherited trait, but it is definitely an acquired characteristic. Contrary to what some think, one need not go all the way to total victory or the finish line or graduation before gaining self-assurance. A person does not struggle until finally confidence is bestowed upon her like a blue ribbon or diploma. She gains it in small, wonderfully enabling doses. Acquiring confidence is not unlike getting into shape physically. The first awkward efforts are painful but become the basis for extending oneself further and enlarging capacity. Confidence is cumulative.

If a woman realizes that confidence will build slowly, she will not be as likely to panic in the face of necessary decisions. A widow or divorcee with limited experience in financial dealings can be dismayed by the necessity of handling such concerns. Though she has no confidence, she has no choice either! Her early decisions about money matters may seem difficult, yet her uncomfortable feelings may only stem from lack of experience with financial matters.

If she is willing to keep learning and deciding, her expertise will grow along with self-confidence. Sometimes widows have already ascertained this by conducting the business affairs of a seriously ill spouse through power of attorney. It is one of the many advantages that power of attorney offers. In any case, a widow will be the beneficiary of a tax windfall since there is no inheritance tax on property transferred to a spouse. This so-called marital tax deduction means that she could have a sizeable portion of the family's assets to manage, perhaps for many years. Eventually she will have to decide how to order family financial affairs for the next generation as well.

The key to building further confidence seems to lie in taking actions. As she proceeds, a woman builds a store of reliable experience that she can apply to a variety of situations and that will support her through hard times. A woman need not have had direct experience in a given area to be able to face it with a confident mind. This is because, besides being cumulative, confidence is somewhat transferable. When a woman develops competence in one part of her life, that capacity can help her as she encounters new situations. She draws upon her reservoir of confidence to make decisions or take action, knowing that nothing valuable in human experience is ever really lost to a person.

Although the gaining of confidence is mostly a gradual process, sometimes it leaps ahead, usually when one takes some big step. Diane related such a gain. After wanting to become a pilot for years, she had signed up for instruction at a local flying school. "I enjoyed everything about my lessons," she said, "until I realized that the goal was for me to solo. I thought I'd have to quit because I did not believe I could take that Cessna up into the air alone. When I finally did solo, it seemed to loosen a tremendous knot of something right here." She pointed to her breastbone. "Strength spread through my whole body. I didn't lose that strength either, once I was back on terra firma."

These comments raise the matter of taking risks. Decision makers usually prefer to avoid risky choices, but that is not always possible or even desirable. A decision that involves significant change usually carries an element of risk. Moreover, a woman who has followed the process of deciding outlined in this study will have become keenly aware of these risks. Lesley was very candid in revealing to a workshop that deciding whether to get married was not an easy choice for her. Another member of the group seemed surprised by her revelation. "Why is that such a tough decision?" she asked Lesley. "Most people in this country do get married." Lesley's reply was that far too many also get divorced.

Lesley went into detail about the risk that a happy, independent, single woman takes when she changes her marital status. "Everything seems so right for me now. I have really made progress with the company. We're starting a new program that I worked hard to get approved. In fact, there is nobody who can do this job the way I can. I hate to think about the possibility of having everything I've worked for disrupted. I happen to like my life the way it is now very much. Is marriage worth risking all that?" Sometimes today a woman uses years of singleness in young adulthood to clarify her ideas about choosing a marital partner or to develop a sense of what a good marriage could mean. Sometimes, like Lesley, her vocation takes on increasing importance during that time. If she is honest, she will admit that this priority could make a satisfactory marriage unlikely. On the other hand, some single women who know themselves well admit that they are likely to feel recriminations later in life if they remain single permanently.

How can an individual incorporate the risk factor into decision making? Psychiatrists point out how hard it is for a person to accept the risk that goes with change or growth. Like others of his profession, Dr. Scott Peck emphasizes this problem in his widely read book, *The Road Less Traveled.* Peck acknowledges that fear makes it difficult for an individual to accept this risk, yet he comes down on the side of risking to make a change or a fresh start. Peck believes that God helps people wanting to change and enlarge their lives. After a long and intense search, the author came to believe in "a powerful force originating outside of human consciousness which nurtures the spiritual growth of human beings."[1] Opening one's life to the power that this psychiatrist came to know is one way of handling the risk factor in decision making.

Peck's hard won belief echoes testimony of Christians stretching back across centuries to the early church. The apostle Paul knew firsthand the extent to which God could transform the life and efforts of a single individual. Seeking somehow to put this truth into words, Paul asserted in the eighth chapter of Romans that in everything God is at work for good with believing people. The power that St. Paul described in this extraordinary passage of Scripture still transforms individuals today. Their faith in God can impel them past deep fear of risk. With faith's vision a woman may come to see how a loving God can bring her through transitions into new and surprising dimensions of living. Taking a risk does leave one vulnerable to pain and disappointment. It can also open the way to joy and enlarge one's capacity for love.

Faith in God's power and help, then, becomes a kind of master key that opens a variety of doors onto a person's future. It would be hard to overstate the role that faith can play in the outcome of decisions. For example, faith can enable an adolescent to see that the future need not be like the past has been for her. As a young teenager starts to grow up, she needs close ties outside her family, though relationships with peers can be problematic. A girlfriend can betray her confidence. A boy's feelings can change or his emotions be difficult for her to judge. It only takes one or two bad experiences for a sensitive adolescent to raise her guard and become cynical about relationships. The gift of faith will keep a teenager seeking dependable friends and caring, compatible boys to enjoy.

In our result-oriented culture, it is not easy today to make a decision largely on faith. People want a "sure thing." Given this cultural bias, it is hardly surprising that personal decisions sometimes reflect a lack of faith or reveal a willingness to write off the future too easily. People do not wish to act without some evidence that the choice will turn out well. Yet any woman who takes a little time to check her own family history and her national or religious heritage will soon realize how faith carried people forward in the past. Some important steps did not seem justified at the time. The individuals taking these actions had absolutely no assurance that the step would turn out at all—much less be significant. Perhaps they were scoffed at and considered foolish. Looking back on such deeds, one wonders if God did not love the faith of these forebears more than their accomplishments.

Faith allows a decision maker to move ahead before she can see ahead. A displaced homemaker with few marketable skills needs a job. A high school graduate requires financial assistance to complete her education. Both must devise plans and act without a guarantee of success. They must make inquiries and believe that other steps will follow their first tentative move. A man and woman struggle to decide about their commitment to one another. Faith impels these single individuals eventually to become the core of a family. A single woman way past forty would like to leave her job and start her own small business. Her faith will be the ingredient in the enterprise that her potential creditors may not account for and marketing experts could overlook.

Finally, a decision maker watches in Step 4 for a sense of rightness to emerge. Go back to the questions posed at the beginning of this chapter. How does a woman know that it is the right time to take action? If she has followed the suggestions in this book, she may have gained a measure of assurance about the process of choosing. She will have clarified both priorities and relationships. She should perceive a general direction and recognize factors that could impede progress toward her goal. All of the preceding three steps can build toward assurance that the time is right for the decision.

One also gains a sense of rightness about decisions by taking a broad view of life. A woman with this perspective knows that human existence consists of ups and downs, of joys and pain. She blends the thinking of the writer of Ecclesiastes into her own outlook. There will be a time for making a fresh start as well as a time for holding back. One has opportunities to realize a gain and also experiences moments of great loss. The process of deciding heightens one's sense of right times and brings a woman into closer touch with the rhythms of existence. A woman with sensitivity and a broad view of life stands a better chance of feeling right about her decisions.

She is mindful that while her efforts have produced an informed decision, her perspective is limited at this point. The passage of time gives a different sense of events and turning points. A person may not yet know all of the ways that God is at work in a situation. Some cannot readily be seen until years have passed. A decision maker knows that often in life the results rest on forces and circumstances beyond the control of an individual. Thus she is able to feel right about deciding without comprehending the implications fully. People with open hearts seem able to receive an affirmation of rightness which they can only partially explain.

This happened with a woman named Sue who had become quite unsettled in her early sixties. She felt altogether unwilling to accept that she had done as much as possible with her life and grew determined to launch a new phase. All of this momentum confounded her husband who was on the brink of retirement, frightened her elderly mother, and confused her children. Sue had a clutch of friends who supported her enthusiastically but worried about her state of mind on occasion. Then one day Sue told her support group of waking up in the night and gaining this feeling of rightness. "I sensed that all this itch and agony I've been through lately was totally known and understood. God understood that Sue Larson had had to work through this dilemma because of the way she is. And now God had brought Sue Larson through it. Oh, that's not all I felt. And the whole thing lasted maybe two minutes. I fell asleep again. But next morning when I got up and moved around, I felt different."

An encounter with God can bring a sense of rightness about decisions even though it is not easy to explain to family and friends. The individual knows that whatever happens could turn out to be right in a way that is sometimes beyond the limit of her understanding at that moment. Such an experience can also bring affirmation of one's worth as a person. A woman like Sue is reassured that her being alive matters in some way. An encounter with God can start a strange trustfulness growing within the most frightened or despondent soul. It is subtle and quiet but within easy reach of her consciousness. It builds into a steadying force in her life. Her vision of the future is limited, but she moves ahead entrusting that future to God.

Feeling grateful for the whole of life can help a woman to choose, act, decide, or change. She accepts the givens that come from the past but is open to the possibility that the future may not be like the past. She feels grateful for both. People who are able to maintain a sense of gratitude for the gift of living seem to view their decisions and choices through this prism. They do not have a superficial or false interpretation of life. They never deny the certainties of pain, trouble, or disappointment, and they admit that it is not easy to maintain a sense of gratitude for life when terrible adversity or difficulties come. Yet they seem to remain in better balance and accept the need to act regardless of circumstances. They also reveal on occasion a measure of courage in their decisions. We will move next to look at why courage plays such an important role in decision making.

Going a Step Further:

1. Review the lifeline which you made for chapter 3. Note occasions when you delayed making a decision or taking a necessary action. How did your procrastination affect the outcome?
2. What is the worst encounter with sexism you have experienced?
3. Read Donald Roy Morse and M. Lawrence Furst, *Women Under Stress* (New York: Van Nostrand Reinhold Co., 1982) or Helen DeRosis, *Women and Anxiety* (New York: Delacorte Press, 1979) and consider stressors in your life.
4. Profile the influence of the "significant others" in your life.

9

THE ROLE OF COURAGE
IN DECISION MAKING

Readers might well ask, Is it really appropriate to devote an entire chapter of such a short book to courage? The answer, emphatically, is Yes! It is necessary to examine the meaning of courage in some detail because of its special relationship to our subject. Decision making and change can produce strong inner conflict and complicate the external conditions of one's life. Courage is essential, then, if a woman is to see through her crisis or succeed at her fresh start. Also, because their decisions occur against a backdrop of rapid societal change, women need courage all the more. Pressures of present-day living are especially trying for women. Until the collective consciousness catches up with the new realities, women will face a multitude of difficult choices. Though innovative methods of coping have helped, a fresh acquaintance with courage could be beneficial too.

If decision makers are to make good use of courage, they must understand the attribute better. Misunderstandings have arisen because, in history and literature, courage is often associated with males who performed some daring exploit. Explorers like Christopher Columbus or Admiral Robert Peary are honored for their courage. Their female contemporaries in fifteenth-century Spain and turn-of-the-century America are not equally praised in books for enduring hardships, surmounting obstacles, and triumphing in the end.

Moreover, courage has long-standing association with combat or other dangerous circumstances typically involving males. One of the easiest ways to gain a place in the chronicle of a people or nation is to show bravery in battle or gallantry under fire. Aggression and force have characterized the behavior of the dominant sex since quite early in history. Human males prized the ability to stand firm in danger, called it courage, and claimed that it exemplified manliness. This cultural bias still makes it difficult for women to move past these mythic images of courage. However, a truer understanding can bolster modern women (and men as well).

Courage is not synonymous with fearlessness. On the contrary, it often means taking necessary action while afraid. Journalist Jory Graham, who shared her long struggle with cancer with readers across America, wrote about courage in her syndicated column more than once. Graham hoped that her comments would help people who had been misled about the true meaning of courage. When she once confessed to a friend how frightened she was, the friend countered that she was also showing great courage.

Graham realized that to have courage was to take action despite fears; to go on when one would rather give up. She was always open about her fears. Like Jory Graham, many of the women depicted in this study felt frightened and wondered if they might not be unable to act. Nevertheless, they found the courage to take the steps necessary to assure their own well-being and security. Many probably would deny that they exhibited courage. Some said that they were "scared to death the whole time." They learned, however, as Graham had, that a woman need not rid herself of fear in order to act effectively and courageously.

Courage enables someone to take that first (dreaded) step. For countless women trying to decide or make a fresh start, the first move will be the hardest. The courage they claim at that time will keep them moving. Like gaining confidence, finding one's courage is gradual rather than all-at-once. The example of Ann applies to every person who suspects she has a medical problem and needs the courage to face finding out what is wrong. Ann struggled alone with depression that hung on. She assumed that psychiatric treatment was the only option that could lift the gloom darkening all her life, yet she was afraid of being labeled a "crazie" if she chose that course.

At last Ann found the courage to go to her family physician, even though she concealed the real reason for the visit and complained of problems with her legs. Cautiously she worked her true fears into their conversation and waited breathlessly, expecting to be referred to a psychiatrist. Ann was astonished to hear the doctor say that they would schedule a complete physical for her and some special tests. She learned that the root of her depression might be physiological rather than psychological. Ann would have to wait to learn the diagnosis but felt better able to deal with whatever it might be. She knew that she was going to have professional help. That was preferable to simply remaining afraid. Though dread of disease is a real and sometimes powerful force, courage is powerful too. Its less obvious character can start someone moving to seek treatment before it is too late.

Courage is also a counterbalance to suffering. Women suffer grievously when, for example, intimate relationships are severed by death, divorce, or change of heart. Just as courage may be effective while a person is still fearful, it can help with painful personal loss, too. Loretta had left a husband who had been difficult for years and had become abusive. As she talked about her life, it was clear that domestic violence necessitates courageous choices. Conflict within a household leads to violence more often than Americans like to imagine. It takes many forms from assault, rape, or incest to murder. Previously an almost unmentionable subject, family violence recently has received varying kinds of publicity and this fresh attention promises to generate action. More shelters are being opened for victims. Counseling opportunities are increasing. It is to be hoped that prosecution of those who attack relatives will intensify.

Nevertheless, Loretta's conversation revealed why victims of domestic violence require real courage: they are vulnerable in so many ways. Loretta and her husband were married as teenagers. Through the years she had forgiven the man so much that she could hardly imagine completely cutting her ties to him for her own welfare. When a person is attacked by a stranger on the street, that victim has no qualms about complaining to the police. If a woman is brutalized by someone she knows intimately, however, the decision to call authorities for help is altogether different. Like Loretta, battered wives return to a repentant husband again and again. Children remain silent about sexual molestation or beatings from an authority figure in the household.

Loretta talked further about life without her husband, and her words manifested the courage required to take actions that were clearly in her best interest, even necessary for her safety. She was very uncomfortable with the notion of freedom and found it dismaying to be on her own. Then the conversation shifted to the subject of ending relationships and learning to let go. She said she would never have found the courage to leave if she had not believed that this long part of her life was valid but definitely ended. Sometimes now, she added, when she explained her "story" to someone, the years had a "long-ago-and-far-away" quality that surprised her. Loretta's courage kept her from bitterly turning inward and withdrawing into her pain.

Courage is also called for when a woman needs to readjust relationships with those closest to her. She knows that a change or a fresh start would help, yet she worries about what will happen if the significant other turns a deaf ear. Can she find the courage to act in the face of family opposition? She might risk further damage to an already weakened relationship. Terry was a fifty-year-old wife who deeply wanted to bring back joy into her sexual life while somehow doubting that she deserved the pleasure.

She expressed much pessimism about her marriage. Both she and her husband were busy, responsible people. The union was stable, but it was dull. Yet, at a time when so many marriages were crashing into ruin, how could she risk the safe but joyless status quo? She was afraid that her solid-citizen husband would be offended if she questioned their relationship. Terry said that, from her perspective, their everyday life had become altogether gray. She added that perhaps this was all she could expect at her age. She wondered how a couple like her and her husband could reach a point of consciously choosing joy and pleasure and caring?

Courage *can* help a woman come to terms with her sexuality. Sometimes choices in this area seem to come naturally, or at least they are not accompanied by great conflict. Some individuals succeed in establishing relations at all levels with the opposite sex. Often, however, a woman's sexuality is a source of turmoil, even guilt, rather than satisfaction. The stage of sexual awakening, for example, can be a time of strong feelings that frighten and confuse many adolescents. Teenagers wish to be accepted by peers. No girl wants to be thought of as frigid or a freak, so she dreads being confronted with a choice either of behaving in a way she inwardly hates or of being ridiculed. It takes courage for a young woman to decide that she will wait for a time when she can relate to a male in all areas of their lives and not merely through casual physical contact.

This same kind of courage will keep a woman moving toward ever fuller understanding of her sexuality. As she reaches adulthood, she will view it as a gift to bless life rather than as a source of shame or unhappiness. Sexuality is surely one of God's great gifts to humankind. It encompasses many blessings: the opportunity to relate to another person in an absolutely unique way; the discovery that love is both constant and always different; the trust that grows from the intimacy of two people who care for one another. All these blessings and more were intended to be enjoyed for a lifetime. However, a single older woman may receive signals from grown children or friends that such considerations are behind her and could be unseemly at her age. An older woman needs courage at times to admit (perhaps even to herself) that her sexual needs are legitimate and that passions can be fulfilled into old age.

The benefits of courage are obvious from the examples in this chapter. Despite this, females are not reared primarily to be courageous. Most women find their courage at times, and some—like Jory Graham—exhibit the quality in extraordinary ways. Courage is not, however, the characteristic prized above all by young women today. Many young women reflect shifting values, attaching increased importance to education and training, for example, in recognition of the need to be economically self-reliant. They value fitness as much as good grooming. Yet the new circumstances of their lives call for giving higher priority to courage. Think, for instance, how much a courageous response will mean when women encounter discrimination on the job or wish to alter long-standing behavior patterns. Courage is vital to decision makers of all ages.

How can a woman strengthen her courage, even if she grew up without thinking much about the trait? Every woman has several sources of encouragement upon which she can draw. First, she can look at her own family history. In doing this she reviews what she knows, then pulls together new information and insight. Focusing on females of past generations, she searches for circumstances in which her foremothers showed courage. No family record lacks such individuals. Nonetheless, we easily overlook inspiring women from our own heritage. Too often family history is told in terms of tragedy or catastrophe. Why not revise it to highlight occasions when women persevered, solved problems, made a comeback? An individual need not have full literary evidence to appreciate these positive examples of grit and stamina, of triumph over trouble and sorrow.

Starting with those she actually knows and going back to forebears she has only heard and read about, a woman may gain courage to face the future. The phenomenal impact of the book and subsequent film, *Roots*, demonstrates how a strong family heritage can encourage an individual. One does not need to fantasize about the past or flirt with ancestor worship. Having a knowledge of courageous foremothers is simply a help when a woman needs to stand firm or recover her balance. Amnesia is one of the most terrible mental afflictions, yet many women forfeit the affirmation and encouragement which could be theirs by staying in touch with the best of their personal past.

Greater knowledge of family history can also improve one's perspective on present-day troubles. When contemporary problems loom large, it is well to recall hazards and hardships of our grandmothers, great-grandmothers, and their mothers. Life was of-

ten cut short. Conditions in the workplace were relatively dangerous and oppressive. Preparing for the birth of a child meant
accepting high risk to one's own life and seeing the baby face
deadly illnesses. Legal and social curtailment of personhood were
almost overwhelming. Foremothers who persisted and triumphed
can give one new heart.

Second, women can look beyond their own kinfolk to find encouragement in the national heritage. One of the most exciting efforts of recent feminist scholarship has been to reconstruct
women's experiences in the American past. Heretofore, historical
accounts dwelled on such things as battles, presidents, and court
cases. Books offered little insight into ordinary lives, particularly
those of women. Scholars have corrected this failing. From private
documents such as diaries and letters as well as public documents
like newspapers, they have produced moving and informative accounts of the experiences of American women. The courage of
frontier women, for instance, matched and sometimes surpassed
that of their men. They had to leave behind every familiar part of
life and go into unknown, often hostile, territory. Early American
women had to be brave, or they did not survive.

One's religious heritage can be an additional source of courage.
Feminists of many eras have struggled to come to grips with the patriarchal culture of the Judeo-Christian tradition. From women's legal and social status as property in the Old Testament to the
misogyny of the early Church Fathers, the record is enough to scare
off any self-respecting female. As with earlier feminist movements,
present-day activists sometimes warn women about this religious
tradition. It gave them no legitimacy in the past and presently
seems ambivalent about sexist language and organization. Why not
turn away then and reject this heritage? The ministry of Jesus is an
important reason. Jesus opened a way to God that clearly was intended for all people, not just males. When he shared our time and
space, Jesus demonstrated God's love and concern for all
humankind.

Jesus related to women in unheard of ways. Defying practices
of the day, he seemed ready to treat them as persons. Jesus
healed and instructed females, and they worked in his ministry,

receiving the promise of salvation as readily as male believers. Apparently women retained a strong position in the apostolic church at first. Christianity gained converts because women received different treatment in the fellowship than in other groups of the Hellenistic world. Then, for a number of reasons, the spirit of equality that afforded women opportunities in the early church died during the second century. Thus while Scripture overall records subordination of women, stories of transformed, courageous lives are scattered throughout the New Testament. Even in the Old Testament women sometimes refused to be put down or oppressed. Sarah, Miriam, and others showed nerve, *chutzpah*. Their example shines still today.

People of the ancient exodus, searching for the promised land, were often commanded by God to be of good courage. This scriptural message stands. Wandering confused and afraid, these followers of God had an unfailing presence to guide and uphold them. The Bible offers other words to persons who feel weak and fearful. The Psalms are laced with encouraging passages. Some are direct while others are couched in rich imagery. One translation of Psalm 27:14 reads, "Wait for the LORD; be strong, and let your heart take courage; yea, wait for the LORD!" More recently the command to "Wait for the LORD" has been translated as "Trust in the LORD" (TEV).

Feminists have always been concerned about women relying solely on sexist images of God. Masculine ideas and language, they point out, perpetuate patriarchal elements of Judaism and Christianity. Feminists believe that old-fashioned notions of patriarchy also accentuate passive tendencies in women. Yet there are plenty of images of God that are neither sexist nor anthropomorphic. The Psalms are filled with representations of a Being that breaks into the ordinariness to confront and empower individuals. The psalmist often tells of taking shelter in a mighty rock, an image which modern translators have described as finding a place of refuge, protection. This thought suggests an undergirding and foundation for life—a level of support that keeps one from falling.

Psalm 139 contains a striking image with which to buttress one's courage. The psalmist suggests that a person lives in the hands of

God. This figure of speech is a beautiful reminder of God's providence which a reader can use to gain encouragement. Verses 9 and 10 state, "If I take the wings of the morning and dwell in the uttermost parts of the sea, even there thy hand shall lead me, and thy right hand shall hold me." In another verse the psalmist declares, "Thou dost beset me behind and before, and layest thy hand upon me" (Ps. 139:5). A woman can close her eyes and let the images from this ancient song fill her consciousness: God's hands, preventing her from going under or falling apart; God's hands, pushing her away from a past of sorrow, disappointment; God's hands, leading her into a future one step at a time. Though God is spirit, not flesh, humans have always depended on familiar images to deepen their understanding of the Holy One.

The imagery of this Psalm can be especially meaningful to a woman. She thinks of the most precious thing she ever handled. Perhaps it was a small baby. A mother knows how to place her hands on her baby. She soothes it, assures the child that all is well. At one time or another, every person also handles an inanimate object that has precious meaning. It may be an old silver cup, burnished with use; a faded quilt softened from years of warming and protecting generations of kinfolks; a tablecloth with embroidered brightness unfaded though the needleworker has long gone back to God. Any woman can recall how it felt to handle a cherished bit of cloth or precious metal. In the same way the spirit of God holds a person who fears she may not have the courage to see through a crisis. The support strengthens her trembling legs. The push keeps her from halting. The guidance directs her away from dark places to new situations that are vital and promising.

True courage is closely related to hope, another quality which is frequently misrepresented. A woman struggling against despair or helplessness cannot accept the breezy, easy optimism that sometimes passes for hope. She won't increase her courage by trying to play Pollyanna. Yet there is a kind of hope that does bolster courage and can help one resist the temptation of despair. It will encourage a woman to outlive a conviction that no one cares if she is alive, much less hurting. Theologian Jürgen Moltmann calls this "hope with open eyes, which sees the suffering and yet believes in the future." Moltmann reveals how, as a prisoner of war, he had "a rebirth to new life thanks to a hope for which there was no evidence at all." While in captivity the German scholar experienced "misery and forsakenness and daily humiliation." Withal, he realized he was "not sinking into the abyss" but was "being held up from afar."[1] Moltmann became a Christian because he discovered God in his desolation and learned that God was with him even in the worst experiences.

This is the biblical hope—a force that makes one wise. It is the power that St. Paul ranked as one of the three greatest spiritual gifts. Such hope precedes courage and energizes it. It starts a person toward regaining interest in life. In his letter to Christians in Rome St. Paul returned to the theme of hope again and again. In the eighth chapter, verses 24–25, he wrote, "Now to see is no longer to hope: why should a man endure and wait for what he already sees? But if we hope for something we do not yet see, then, in waiting for it, we show our endurance" (Romans 8:24–25, New English Bible). Paul urged his readers in Romans 12:12, "Let your hope keep you joyful, be patient in your troubles, and pray at all times" (TEV). Hope is God's gift and a source of courage in all of life.

An attitude of thankfulness often underlies hope and strengthens courage as well. A physician who did genetic counseling talked about such an outlook in connection with her work. The couples whom she counseled sometimes experienced a crisis of hope. The husband and wife came to her in the first place out of worry over something in their family history. What might happen, they wondered, if pregnancy occurred? Pregnancy has been helped, the doctor explained, yet also complicated, by new medical knowledge. Tests, such as amniocentesis and a new kind of biopsy, identify serious abnormalities in a fetus. If the results of such tests are positive, the pregnant woman must decide about an abortion, a harrowing choice.

A genetic counselor may even confront a couple with hard choices before pregnancy occurs. With preliminary data at hand, the woman may know the odds of bearing a baby afflicted with defective genes. She and her husband could be forced to search for ways to become a family somehow without a child of their own. A woman who decides to forego motherhood for whatever reason may need special courage to deal with inner conflict, the "empty womb" syndrome. Insensitive family members or acquaintances could intimate that she will remain "unfulfilled." She and her husband will need to take a broad view of life to confirm the rightness of their decisions. If she can give thanks for the whole of living and cling to hope, she may keep her courage despite feeling confused and afraid.

The Bible is filled with scenes of courageous thanksgiving in the midst of difficulty. In the dramatic climax to the book of Acts, Luke describes Paul's final voyage to Rome to appeal to Caesar. Through months of storm and other threats Paul maintained his courage by thankfulness. Safely on land at last, they approached the long-sought destination. At the edge of the imperial city, Luke records, their party was met by some Christians who heard of their coming. When Paul saw them, he gave thanks to God and took courage. To the end of his life the imprisoned apostle was filled with gratitude for the life God had given him. Thus freed from fear, Paul found possibilities for witness until he died. In letters to the churches, Paul urged believers to have a thankful heart. They were never to doubt that God would provide whatever courage they needed to triumph over trials. They were, he said in Philippians 4:6, to ask God to meet their needs with "a thankful heart" (TEV).

Courage is crucial to putting the past behind and moving with joy toward an unknown future. At some point all the tortured questions have been asked. Regrets have been spelled out silently and to anyone who will listen. Denial of the problem no longer works. Decision makers know that when they reach this point only courage will help. Everyone must find the courage to go on from there. It is inescapable. This is why decision makers must understand the true meaning of courage. It is the secret to believing that the future will not be like the past has been and then formulating plans based on that belief.

In a workshop, Patty, a teacher in her mid-thirties, talked about the courage necessary to starting anew. She had recently become a single parent and faced an almost overwhelming series of decisions. None seemed to worry her more than the fear that, in the years ahead, she could never reconcile her own needs with demands of job and her children. Other members of the group listened and shared with Patty their varying struggles with that particular tangle of pressures experienced by working wives and mothers. Popularly known as the "Superwoman syndrome," the behavior pattern is exhibited by a woman who somehow believes she can excel both on the homefront and on the job.

The "Superwoman syndrome" is a special temptation for contemporary females who are highly motivated and very able. A decade or so ago many women assumed that, if they were efficient enough, they could capitalize fully on new opportunities in the workplace without missing the joys of motherhood. Most have since discovered that Superwoman truly does not exist. Real-life situations bear no resemblance to comic strip fantasies. Nevertheless, working mothers know all too well that it is no easy matter to cast off the "Superwoman syndrome." Conscientious and determined to prove their worth, they are tempted to try to squeeze more and more work into longer waking hours. They feel obliged to labor every bit as hard at home as at their place of employment. Like Patty, they often bear most of the parental responsibility.

It takes strong courage to stop playing "Superwoman." First, a woman has to accept that her energy and ability truly are limited. Patty admitted that for years she had been fiercely determined to be super at everything she did and to try almost anything. Sometimes a woman gives up the "Superwoman" role for health's sake. She may be presented with a choice of developing a stress-related medical problem or foregoing a behavior pattern to which she has become addicted. Patty told the group of reading a book that explained how the adrenaline release in a driven, overworked individual can become almost a physiological dependency. In a sense, Patty continued, she was a work addict. She had also read some of the growing evidence linking stress to health problems from coronaries to cancer. Patty told the others how she had learned to recognize adverse signs of stress in her own life. She knew that statistically women workers are beginning to exhibit the vulnerability to job-related ills that males have previously shown. These range from hypertension to heart disease. Her health was not yet impaired, but Patty was beginning to fear that it might suffer if she continued to play "Superwoman."

Even if a woman strongly wishes to abandon this behavior pattern, she will have to deal with individuals in her household and at work who have come to rely on her workaholism. First she must tell all of these persons that she is not able to do everything; then she must persuade them that she no longer intends to try. Heretofore, she went "all out" all of the time. Now they must accept limits she wishes to set. They will have to learn to honor her intention to hold back, to choose pleasure over duties.

A reformed "Superwoman" may have more difficulty establishing a new pattern with those at home than with her fellow employees. As Patty said, the last emotion a single parent needs is guilt. However, as she thought back over the past months, she wondered why she had not exploded into a thousand pieces. She resolved to begin balancing responsibility for work on the homefront. The others convinced Patty that her children would benefit from sharing domestic chores. They would develop a sense of responsibility and grow up knowing that they were making a genuine contribution to the family. Patty began to see how to begin her fresh start.

In the same workshop an elderly and very frail woman shared how one's courage is enhanced by a sense throughout life of going toward God. She had decided to participate in the workshop because she wished to take steps to become less vulnerable during the remainder of her life. She had considered a change of residence, alarm systems, a daily calling service, a new physician. Beneath her discussion of these choices lay deeper, unspoken fears which she addressed in the follow-up session. She said she really wondered whether her life meant all that it should. Where was this increasingly feeble existence leading? How would it end? Was she strong enough to stand up to whatever lay ahead? She was, she admitted, most afraid of just going into some unknown realm.

Then, in solitary reading of Scripture, she had found an affirmation of life's meaning. She read two passages to our group. The first was from 2 Corinthians. "So we do not lose heart. Though our outer nature is wasting away, our inner nature is being renewed everyday. . . . For we know that if the earthly tent we live in is destroyed, we have a building from God, a house not made with hands, eternal in the heavens. . . . So we are always of good courage; we know that while we are at home in the body we are away from the Lord" (2 Cor. 4:16; 5:1,6). Then she read, "The LORD is my shepherd; I have everything I need. He lets me rest in fields of green grass and leads me to quiet pools of fresh water. He gives me new strength. He guides me in the right paths, as he has promised. Even if I go through deepest darkness, I will not be afraid, LORD, for you are with me" (Psalm 23:1–4, TEV). In God a person finds the courage to face the varying conditions of life to the very end.

Going a Step Further:

1. Write a family history in terms of courageous behavior or comeback stories.
2. Read Lillian Schlissel, comp., *Women's Diaries of the Westward Journey* (New York: Schocken Books, 1982) or Joanna L. Stratton, *Pioneer Women: Voices from the Kansas Frontier* (New York: Simon & Schuster, 1981) and note the contrast to contemporary lives.
3. Read Marjorie Hansen Shaevitz, *The Superwoman Syndrome* (New York: Warner Books, 1984) and discuss specific suggestions for a woman like Patty to relinquish the role of "Superwoman."
4. Read Sharon Neufer Emswiler and Thomas Neufer Emswiler, *Women & Worship: A Guide to Non-Sexist Hymns, Prayers, and Liturgies* (New York: Harper & Row, 1974) and consider ways to make use of inclusive language in worship.

10

A NEW VIEW OF
THE FUTURE

Going through the process of decision making enables women to see the importance of taking a broad view. This experience with planning, envisioning, and acting purposefully helps them appreciate the power of initiative. As women begin to establish a measure of control over the private areas of their lives through strong personal decisions, they often gain a sense of possibilities for acting effectively in the public realm. Those who have become accustomed to utilizing the decision-making steps for private matters gain enlarged vision.

They see that the same framework can be expanded to help secure the common future. Realism about the givens, creative vision, information gathering, and action are as relevant to corporate concerns as they are to individual dilemmas. Moreover, as women confront these communal problems, their efforts are being influenced by a new view of the future. Drawing upon their traditional past and recent, transitional experiences, women are developing a promising approach to these larger challenges.

What are some of the signs that encourage us to hope that women will act effectively to ameliorate threats to the future? First, they now know that they have the power to bring about political and social change. In the past women led relatively private lives. A few courageous, singular individuals tried to influence public concerns. However, women were excluded from the exercise of economic power and barred from political activism. The history of the female sex is, by and large, the record of a subjugated minority. That circumstance recently changed.

Women are presently in the majority in America and are in a potentially strong position to initiate change. They no longer perceive themselves—individually and collectively—as being powerless. They understand that their numbers could translate into votes and political pressure, for example. In recent American history people have deplored trends and technological innovations that make them feel more like a number than a person. Much gloomy comment has been voiced that we all stand in danger of becoming mere statistics. One woman complained, "Nobody seems to know us anymore, only our number. At the bank, with my store credit cards, everywhere. Nobody cares what my name is, but they all need to have my number." Rather than giving in to such pessimism, many women are working to turn their numbers into economic and social reforms.

This new reality is leading women to become well informed about many public issues and to demonstrate that they are able and willing to attack these problems actively. In fact, it is possible that women will play a very special role in contending with some of the nation's fundamental social questions. For example, America promises justice, equality, and opportunity to its citizens, yet inequities abound. The struggle to close this gap between public ideals and actualities goes forward in legislative bodies, corporate board rooms, and within households. With a sensitivity to discrimination and oppression as well as a traditional sense of responsibility for nurturing, women can spearhead efforts to fulfill these age-old promises.

Having experienced unfairness and suffering, women are sensitive to the plight of other victims. They can see troubled and neglected people who might be overlooked. They will not turn away in judgment from prisoners, migrant workers, or prostitutes. Women can search for ways to offer weak groups in society new opportunity and humane treatment. Children are especially vulnerable. One in five American children now lives in situations officially classified as poor. The figure for Black children is one in two. How can the future of the country be considered "secure" if the health, nutritional, and educational needs of these children go unmet?

Another sign that women could be instrumental in securing the future is the tremendous attitudinal shift underway both among women and about women. The well-marked endeavor of women to become persons in their own right takes shape politically, economically, and psychologically. Women are voting in growing numbers. In the election of 1980 a greater percentage of female voters than males went to the polls for the first time, and in 1984 their participation increased to perhaps 60 percent of the ballots cast. Mass movement of women into the work force has affected their opinion of many socioeconomic issues, including various government policies that are likely to affect their well-being. Moreover, between 1970 and 1974, according to a Roper poll, the percentage of men and women favoring efforts to strengthen or change women's status in society increased from 44–63 percent and 40–57 percent respectively. A public opinion sample taken by Louis Harris in 1972 revealed that 71 percent of American women believed they should speak up and do something about their status.

It would be naive to assume that reforms will follow easily from these changing attitudes. Most social issues are quite complex. Public opinion is fragmented, even on some matters that affect women directly and profoundly. Moreover, many Americans have become cynical about prospects for affecting governmental policies. Meaningful debate of alternatives seldom seems to occur. Some substantive policies are made through a process that is veiled in secrecy because of executive agreements or security considerations. Government sometimes seems to proceed without real regard for the will or the wishes of average Americans. Even the election proceedings appear to be contrived and dominated by media.

Despite these negative factors, there is cause for hope. In the first place, those wishing to change or initiate policies are dealing with a republican form of government at the local, state, and national levels. It is easy to condemn or criticize what THEY are doing in Washington, the state capital, or county seat. In truth, however, the government is not THEY but WE. The fact is that anti-democratic elements in government, such as those mentioned above, can only be eliminated by more democracy. If citizens will renew their sense of responsibility and increase active involvement in the process of governing, the system can be revitalized. When women and men take the time and trouble to participate, government responds to their direction.

A third encouraging sign that women may be poised to help secure the future comes from the evolution of feminism itself. The recent movement for women's equality sparked sharp controversy over the differences between the sexes. In its early phase the movement produced a feeling that women must renounce so-called feminine qualities. In order to advance the cause, it was felt, women should adopt attitudes and behavior that would be labeled "masculine." Women wanting to prove that they could compete successfully in a male-dominated culture consciously laid aside "feminine" modes. Feminists also decried scholarship in which lines of inquiry flowed from a concept of a feminine biology. They were afraid that such research would play into the hands of those wishing to limit women's opportunities and even reverse gains already made on their behalf.

Perhaps during the next stage women can reclaim some valuable elements of their cultural and social experience for the new view. The fierce determination to attack discrimination and misogyny that characterized early feminism often produced confrontation and conflict between the sexes. Now men and women show signs of fusing the best qualities which have evolved for each sex into a new ideal. The resulting social construct will combine strong attributes traditionally associated with each sex and omit undesirable ones. At one end of the spectrum of qualities are patterns of aggression and competitiveness. At the other is behavior that is passive and dependent. Neither extreme would be helpful to the new blend. If these warped, sexist elements are abandoned, both men and women can step toward wholeness and integration. Women offer their valuation of social ties, connectedness, and caring to the new view. Men bring their age-old reliance upon action and a desire to shape their environment rationally.

Both sexes are coming to appreciate that the overlapping elements of behavior are the crux of the new view. The species would never have thrived without them. For perhaps as many as 50,000 years men and women *together* have provided the means by which young human beings are protected, survive, and grow up to bear another generation. Any nature/nurture controversy pales beside this great existential truth. Today mothers and fathers sometimes share parenting in ways that enrich the entire family. More often women are the primary child-rearers. In either case, parents have a unique opportunity to influence the thinking of daughters and sons. The result can be changed thinking about subjects from girl-boy relations to nuclear war.

One example makes the point. Television has become a powerful shaping force in the lives of American children. Experts claim that by age sixteen a young person has spent much more time watching television than in school classrooms. They estimate that, on average, a child has consumed 15,000 hours as a TV viewer by his sixteenth birthday. Young people are susceptible to the influence of the "cool medium" in many ways. Through the manipulation of television advertising, they crave clothes, records, cars, and other products.

Young Americans need parental help in dealing with the effects of television. Its advertising entices them to spend money whether necessary or not. However, they must also be able to make sound financial decisions of all kinds. This ability has to develop from childhood. Parents with a new view can also help counter the view of the world that television offers to young audiences. It may be so simplistic and banal that these young people will have difficulty contending with the real world when the time comes. While children are susceptible to television, the media are subject to pressures applied by parents to change programming and even alter advertising.

A fourth hopeful sign of an emerging new view is that women are laying claim to Christian tenets as grounds for taking actions that will promote a fairer, more humane society. When the recent feminist movement gathered momentum, women were often confused about how it fit with Christianity. Questions arose, for example, over whether a woman could become assertive yet remain giving and unselfish. Did the command that Christians turn the other cheek and go the extra mile conflict with demanding one's rights and challenging the status quo? Many women doubted that they could be feminists and traditional Christians at the same time.

Statements by antifeminist religious leaders added to their confusion. As noted at the beginning of this study, such persons urged women to remain within domestic settings (usually subordinate to a male head of family). The trend of working women, they warned, would erode moral values and accelerate family disintegration. Upon reflection, women realized that these antifeminists were wrong. Family life based upon equitable relations and mutuality was far more satisfactory than a basis where wives were dependent, even submissive to their husbands. Couples found that they could create and maintain such a union within the framework of Christianity.

Likewise, women on occasion hesitated to participate in social causes because of certain religious ideas. Christianity has always had a strain whose followers shun involvement in this world and dwell on hopes for the life beyond. This temptation to turn inward runs counter to Jesus' commands and his example. Where there is human need or suffering or injustice of any kind, Christian folk are obliged to combat them. In the parable of the Last Judgment Jesus described specifically what would happen to those who ignored victims of these problems. His teachings are clear about working for the justice of all.

Neither individualism nor privatism are appropriate attitudes for followers of Christ. There is ample biblical basis for getting involved in causes that transcend selfish, private concerns. Besides an obvious emphasis in the Gospels, one finds surprising prescripts in the Old Testament. Proverbs 31 contains a description of an ideal wife. Naturally, she is attentive to the needs and wants of her husband and all of her household. At the same time the "virtuous wife" devotes time and effort to community concerns. She is competent, well informed, and respected. She is clearly an activist for that era. Similarly today, the *shalom*—the peace, health, wholeness for which we long—is fostered by committed, involved women.

Most of all, coming together to act enlarges hope. As we have seen, hope is a scarce commodity in today's world. Nonetheless, hope is one of the cardinal virtues of a Christian. It is seldom easy to feel very hopeful as long as one is alone and undecided about what to do next. When women join forces to work for a goal, however, hope grows. The antidotes to anxiety and fear—joy, hope, and peace—are gifts of God's spirit. From Pentecost to the present, believers have always found that this spirit comes in enabling power when they join together. For this reason and many more, a strong current of Christian feminism operates today, providing a framework for acting to help shape a better society.

One element in this framework is appreciation of the interconnectedness of all life. Every living thing is part of a network, binding humans to one another and all our species to the matter, energy, and other organisms of earth. This web of relationships is scientific fact. We share resources of the biosphere—air, soil, water—with all our fellow creatures. Humans presently have unprecedented power to alter and affect the world, though we are very recent arrivals on the four billion-year-old planet. Creatures such as insects, whose habitation here precedes ours by millions of years and who might succeed humans as the dominant organism, could raise our consciousness about life on earth! Their revelations might shatter our species' self-importance and revive a desire to preserve all life.

The interconnectedness of life has a biblical basis as well as being a scientific reality. Both the Old and New Testaments set forth the view of *oikoumenē*—the whole inhabited earth in God. This vision of a totality has the power to alter one's thinking and behavior. Practices that once seemed justified, conditions that were irritating dwindle in importance when a person understands these larger connections. A suburban American sees her family's lifestyle through the eyes of an African mother whose children are sick and hungry. She grasps how their suffering diminishes her family's existence. She senses that creation is an ongoing process and accepts the possibility that she may have a tiny part to play in insuring a better life for all.

What can draw an individual out of self-centered preoccupations and into the *oikoumenē*? One could begin by reestablishing connections to the natural world, progressing then to social constructs. Few people are immune to the pleasure of being alive under the high blue dome of a fall day. Even someone turned in upon herself quickens with joy walking on the hot, sandy edge of sparkling surf. Going out into a storm, a person is swept up into turbulence and somehow flows into other elements of the physical world. It is then a small, second step to feel at one with much more of the life on planet earth. The lovely ancient prayer of St. Patrick expressed the insight poetically:

I bind unto myself this day
The stable earth, the deep salt sea,
The sweet pale moon, the sun's bright ray,
The whirling winds, the lightning free.

Opening up to the wonders of nature, an individual can build other ties and accept new obligations. When a woman really enjoys part of the physical world, she feels obliged to see that it remains beautiful, safe, able to support abundant life. In time she makes connections to other human inhabitants of earth. She recognizes that all share her need for food, water, shelter. They wish to enjoy their families, work with dignity, and avoid suffering or a catastrophe. Forces that threaten them threaten her as well. She may always prefer the company of people most like her, but she sees that beyond national, cultural, and religious divisions the destiny of earth is one.

A new view of the future also includes a strong sense of community. The early church spread like wildfire in the Hellenistic world because it offered to its converts fellowship within a *koinonia*, a real community. Christians competed successfully with other religions in the apostolic age by accepting one another in the same unconditional way that God had accepted them. Within the fellowship, social and racial divisions blurred. Believers depended upon one another in an era of rapid change, not unlike our own times. Many churches today seek to vitalize the sense of *koinonia*. Members offer support to one another in a spirit that is different from the help individuals receive from professional counselors or therapists.

Signs point to a revived interest in community generally. Americans recognize that "rugged individualism" is inappropriate for the future and probably is an illusion about the country's past. Like early Christians, early Americans had to depend on one another to survive. Historians of American family life are struck by the fact that living arrangements in this century have eroded families' ties to the community. Houses and apartments in America afford much privacy but weaken our sense of interdependency by and large. When, on the other hand, we have vital connections to a genuine community of some sort, those ties nourish many aspects of individual existence.

Two examples attest to the importance of community. When elderly people move into retirement communities from solitary residences, they sometimes show fresh liveliness. They share bits and pieces of their lives with other residents. They are free to participate in everything that is happening. They are part of a larger existence and feel new vitality themselves. The phenomenon of choosing kin also demonstrates the need for community. Blood relatives are often separated by distances and estranged by family failings. Throughout the country, people are creating alternatives to fill the needs that strong kinfolks meet. They establish agreements with close friends or neighbors to take responsibility for one another's family in crisis or tragedy. They share holidays or other meaningful occasions.

Women draw particular strength from being part of a community. Too much isolation puts them at risk to alienation and despair. Alienation is a powerful theme in modern art and literature. It is, moreover, a tragic reality in the lives of far too many women today. Community participation assists a woman with defining and creating a self. It challenges her to be active and responsive to the needs of others within the community. The give-and-take suggests opportunities and directions that she might never see all by herself. Whether the community is a neighborhood, a church, a support group, or an office, it affords life which a woman cannot find on her own.

The new view realizes, in the third place, that earth's creatures survive only if they are able to change. This generation may be fortunate in being forced to respond to much change all at once. To be sure, families have experienced confusion and conflict over recent social changes. Yet upheavals may make us aware of how precarious the continued dominance of humankind really is. Awareness of the inevitability of change also could alert us to take steps that will insure our survival. In the natural world one sees evidence of constant change. We know that when species or populations prove unable to adapt to changing environments they become extinct. Will *Homo sapiens* share the fate of the wooly mammoth and the dinosaurs?

The future is not predetermined, and humankind is not fated for rapid extinction. Earth can continue to support abundant life for eons. However, threats are very real. In the brief period of 25,000 to 50,000 years since humankind came to dominate life on earth, the species has acquired the means to affect the biosphere drastically. *Homo sapiens* is quite numerous. The conflicts and industry of the species could prove catastrophic for all life. The same qualities that gave humankind its dominance can now be turned to the use of preserving the future. The brains that accumulated knowledge, communicated through the unique power of language, and built marvelous tools, can alter dangerous circumstances and bring about constructive change. Surely a species that typically has cared for its young during long dependency and has cooperated in complex societies in order to thrive will not allow the present threats to become its doom.

Yet these threats are serious and challenge this generation to adopt a new way of thinking and acting. It is indisputable that nuclear weapons threaten all life on earth. From its outset in 1945 the nuclear age has provided horrible hints of destruction and a record of death. When Hiroshima was bombed, about 50,000 persons died immediately and 100,000 more suffered often fatal injuries. Over four decades weapons technology has advanced so rapidly that now approximately 40,000 to 50,000 nuclear arms stand ready to be fired, each possessing the destructive capacity of the Hiroshima bomb. Although it is time to think and act, this peril is often described as almost unthinkable. Why?

Partly because such destruction is so hard to comprehend that people decide to avoid facing the threat directly. Also we are too fearful of these doomsday weapons to deal effectively with the problem. Yet human intellect and intent generated the threat, and only rational, active people will remove the menace. As Pope John Paul has said, "from now on, it is only through a conscious choice and then deliberate policy that humanity can survive." In the four decades since the nuclear age dawned billions of dollars and inestimable brainpower have gone into the arms race. It will require perhaps equal effort to deliver humankind from this peril.

Perhaps hope will finally provide us with the motivation to overcome the threat to the planet posed by nuclear holocaust. In his powerful book, *Weapons and Hope,* physicist Freeman Dyson argues that replacing fear with hope could be the critical psychological shift necessary to halting the nuclear arms race. Technically it is possible to abolish weapons and verify violations of disarmament, yet countless people first must attain hope that this process is going to be accomplished politically. However, as the century draws to a close, the tone of public life seems to be fearful rather than hopeful. In fact, fear plays a larger role in U.S. public opinion than is generally acknowledged. In the social, political, and economic realms appeals are often made to underlying fears. Accustomed to being asked to decide on the basis of fears, Americans are missing possibilities to improve conditions—even reverse the arms race. With a shift in public consciousness toward hope, however, the nation could envision a world secure without nuclear arms and move to make that vision a reality.

Scarcity is also a threat. As noted earlier, economic growth has slowed, and prosperity is no longer assured. Earth's natural resources are finite, yet until the energy crisis of 1973–74, industrial economies proceeded as if these raw materials were limitless. Expansion seemed to have no bounds. Now citizens of the United

States, along with other industrialized nations, face the fact that the basis on which the American economy developed for a century and a half is simply no longer viable. For example, fossil fuels, the power source that impelled industrialism up until now, no longer avail. Oil is undoubtedly limited and often under hostile control. Coal is plentiful, but its use seriously threatens the environment. In addition, alternative energy sources will be hard to obtain.

U.S. economic prospects confront Americans with a host of decisions. The economy will affect distribution of wealth in future society. This fact introduces value judgments into discussions that might initially seem to be purely economic. Will, for instance, our citizens share more equally the pieces of an economic pie that may not grow bigger? Or will recent trends of impoverishment accelerate? Decisions about economic policy relate to notions of justice and a decent life for everyone.

Will growing numbers of people earn less and less while a minority of Americans thrive and become wealthy? Between 1978 and 1983 the number of Americans officially classified as poor rose from 24.5 million to 35.3 million. Not only is the status of those at lowest income levels worsening, but some middle-income families also face deteriorating circumstances. From 1978 to 1983 the mid-portion of America's middle class shrank from 55 percent of the population to only 42 percent. Three-quarters of the families changing status declined in income. This shift was due to many factors, none more important than the rising divorce rate. Families in which a single parent headed the household suffered serious drops in real disposable income.

Future security is tied to ecology as well as economy, and scientists warn us to ponder ominous changes there. The planet's biosphere, which sustains all life, is more fragile than people like to think. The fossil fuels that are the underpinning of America's work and residential patterns threaten this biosphere. Their burning has raised carbon dioxide levels and warmed the atmosphere to a point that climate, agriculture, and the economy could be profoundly affected. This "greenhouse effect" could be felt in a decade or so. Unless Americans and other highly developed nations address the problem, it could transform the shape of the future for all peoples.

The earth's environment and natural resources, upon which our well-being depends, are also threatened by chemicals. Safe and ample water supplies in both surface and underground sources are in danger. The groundwater supply is imperiled by the disposal of radioactive wastes and toxic materials. Rivers and lakes can become so polluted that animal life dies. Fertilizers and pesticides have enabled agriculture to increase enormously the output of foodstuffs. However, these substances also pollute our water supplies and pose other risks to health and safety. One must ask whether it will be possible to satisfy the world's growing need for food without damaging ecosystems in many countries around the globe.

Just as economic scarcity calls for wise judgments, so ecological problems point up the commonality of life. All living things need food, water, oxygen. Can the "haves" ignore the plight of the "have-nots" and expect a secure future in a world where problems are global in scope? Americans constitute only 6 percent of the world's population but consume perhaps two-thirds of earth's resources. Do the material comforts and high-energy lifestyles that many Americans enjoy cost too much in the larger scheme of things? What consideration has been given to replacing the ethos of consumerism with one of conservation and restoration? Individuals set priorities when making personal decisions. Cannot entire societies and nation-states identify what is most important? In an age of limits, no country should expect to have its way in every issue, especially when problems are complex and interlocked.

Several demographic shifts, occurring within the United States and in the world at large, could threaten our expectations about the future. Foremost among them is the fact that the number of people living on earth is growing at a staggering rate. Not long ago a researcher estimated that the number of persons alive equaled 10 percent of the total number who had ever lived. The world's population is approaching 5 billion. If the current growth rate continues, the number of people on the earth could double every forty years. The population explosion seems to portend the end of a geopolitical system dominated by two superpowers or even a handful of great powers. With so many human beings crowded on the planet, surely we must devise a different system for handling conflicts that inevitably arise among nations and social groups.

This demographic time bomb threatens the collective future for various reasons. One is the question of food. Agricultural productivity is tied to many other imponderables. Can sufficient food even be produced for these billions? Modern agricultural production is based on oil. Food could be at the center of future conflicts between petroleum-producing states and those that consume oil, whether they are First or Fourth World countries. If famine sweeps through Third and Fourth World nations, will their governments resort to nuclear terrorism or blackmail—holding strategic minerals to obtain food from governments like the United States? Challenges to the future security are indeed interrelated.

Striking demographic changes within Christianity relate to other issues raised in this section. This faith, which is claimed by about 33 percent of the world's population, could soon be changed as dramatically as it was by events in the apostolic age. By the year 2000 more than three-fifths of all Christians will be Africans, Asians, and Latin Americans. This fact will end lengthy domination of the faith by whites. The development will have deep, perhaps wrenching, repercussions on believers in Western Europe and the United States. Moreover, traditional Protestant denominations are not growing nearly as rapidly as the Evangelicals. These sects, dominated by the Pentecostalists, account for a strong majority of all Protestants worldwide. They are also the most active missionaries in many emerging areas of the globe where the faith is gaining converts.

Taken altogether, these developments could give Christianity a form and content that many mainstream American churchgoers would find unfamiliar. Mission efforts as a whole now aim to impose as little Western enculturation with the gospel as possible. They seek to develop rapidly an indigenous structure for Christianity. This stance means giving heed to independent local groups and sometimes bowing to tribal practices. To complicate the picture, missionaries, often Roman Catholics, have enlarged their concern for the poor and downtrodden to advocate radical political and economic change. Sometimes they call for revolution through a "liberation theology."

It is not easy for Christians who sit in "the comfortable pew" to decide how to respond to these trends. "Liberation theology," for example, pleads for releasing people from oppression by whatever means is necessary, yet it also asks for strong commitment to justice. Mainstream Christians are giving all of these global changes serious, prayerful consideration. They recall that the New Testament faith was first proclaimed to poor, oppressed people. Also Jesus commanded that his own ministry to human needs become the model for his disciples thereafter. The destiny which God intends for Christianity could very well disturb our notions of the status quo.

After looking specifically at some of the threatening forces that intersect with our individual lives and considering elements of a new view, it might be well to conclude with two simple imaging exercises. Both could enlarge one's vision of the future. A woman closes her eyes and images first space and then time. She visualizes herself moving out—beyond her home, her neighborhood. She sees the entire community. Then she images the region, the United States, and the western hemisphere. She sees the whole earth, just as space age photography has relayed stunning visual confirmation of our home planet.

Spatial imaging is a powerful way to remind us of how fragile individual life is and how miraculous. The exercise revives our sense of being part of all creation. Ultimately, one must image our place in the solar system, the Milky Way galaxy, the cosmos. In imaging about the physical universe, an individual connects with the Cause behind the entire cosmos. Of course, it is extremely difficult to imagine the size of space. And scientists are probably correct to assert that the universe is mostly dark and empty. We believe that back of it all, however, is the power of creation. Our finite image of that power is blinding, pure, brilliant light—brighter than any of us could behold or imagine.

Next one should try imaging time. This exercise could be harder than visualizing space. After all, we carry some pictures around in our heads whether from geography books or NASA television. While it may seem a formidable task to contemplate future time, the exercise could lead a woman to adopt a new view. She starts by picturing tomorrow, next month, a year from now, twenty years. Then she tries to envision what the world will be like in a century, even a millennium. Perhaps all of her images are based on the assumption of continual change. This is understandable. So much rapid and drastic change has occurred in recent decades that those of us alive today simply assume the future will bring greater change. Yet the future is not really out there. Whatever a person's imaging projects, it is up to her to shape and secure her own future and the common fate.

Going a Step Further:

1. Read Joan Bodner, ed., *Taking Charge of Our Lives: Living Responsibly in the World* (San Francisco: Harper & Row, 1984) and act on one of the many suggestions in this volume.
2. Rewrite Proverbs 31 using a contemporary woman's activities and options instead of Old Testament ones.
3. Read Charlotte Holt Clinebell, *Meet Me in the Middle: On Becoming Human Together* (New York: Harper & Row, 1973) and reconsider relations with the opposite sex.
4. Go back through this chapter's discussion of threats to the future and think about how elements of decision making from chapters 5–8 apply to these challenges.

NOTES

Chapter 4
1. Helen DeRosis, *Women and Anxiety* (New York: Delacorte Press, 1979), 190.
2. Allen Wheelis, *How People Change* (New York: Harper & Row, 1973), 102.
3. M. Scott Peck, *The Road Less Traveled: A New Psychology of Love, Traditional Values and Spiritual Growth* (New York: Simon and Schuster, 1978), 276.

Chapter 7
1. David Baily Harned, *Grace and Common Life*, 1st Am. ed. (Charlottesville: University Press of Virginia, 1971), 70.

Chapter 8
1. Peck, *Road Less Traveled*, 260.

Chapter 9
1. Jürgen Moltmann, *Experiences of God*, trans. Margaret Kohl (Philadelphia: Fortress Press, 1980), 14, 7, 8.

INDEX

singleness, 103–104, 119–120. *See also* parenthood, single
Social Security, 54, 86–87
socialization of females, 10–11, 106–108, 129–130, 142–143
stress, 65, 105, 114–115, 136–137
"Superwoman syndrome," 136–137
support groups, 41–43

time, 21, 46, 57–59, 102, 122; and families, 23, 97–98

vocation, 17–18, 31–32, 36, 105–106
voluntarism, 100

widowhood, 53–54, 75–76, 85–87, 99–100, 111–112, 118–119; and limits, 64, 70–71
women's liberation. *See* feminism